Jihad in Paradise

Jihad in Paradise

❖❖❖

Islam and Politics in Southeast Asia

FOREWORD BY IVAN HALL

Mike Millard

An East Gate Book

M.E.Sharpe
Armonk, New York
London, England

An East Gate Book

Copyright © 2004 by M.E. Sharpe, Inc.

Library of Congress Cataloging-in-Publication Data

Millard, Mike, 1947
    Jihad in paradise : Islam and politics in Southeast Asia / Mike Millard.
        p. cm.
    Includes index.
    ISBN 0-7656-1335-2 (cloth: alk. paper)
    ISBN 0-7656-1336-0 (pbk.: alk. paper)
    1. Terrorism—Asia, Southeastern. 2. Islam and terrorism—Asia,
Southeastern. 3. Jamaah Islamiyah (Indonesia). 4. Jemaah Islamiyah
(Singapore). 5. Jihad. I. Title.
HV6433.A7852 J366 2004
303.6′25′088297′0959—dc22

                                                                    2003023074

Printed in the United States of America

The paper used in this publication meets the minimum requirements of
American National Standard for Information Sciences
Permanence of Paper for Printed Library Materials,
ANSI Z 39.48-1984.

BM (c)   10   9   8   7   6   5   4   3   2   1
BM (p)   10   9   8   7   6   5   4   3   2   1

For the next generation, Alexa, Clarissa, Noah, Cooper, and Emerson, who carry our hopes.

We may with more successful hope resolve
To wage by force or guile eternal Warr
Irreconcileable, to our grand Foe,
Who now triumphs, and in th' excess of joy
Sole reigning holds the Tyranny of Heav'n.

—John Milton

CONTENTS

FOREWORD

Among my fellow expatriate friends in East Asia, I have treasured Mike Millard over the years not only as a conversational companion par excellence, but also as an ebullient and socially gregarious writer with a unique knack for drawing his readers into complex and potentially dry subject matter precisely by means of a narrative thread of intimate conversational interviews that allows individuals caught up in great issues to speak for themselves. And that goes for body language, too—not missing a tic of the head or a pregnant pause, be it from a cabinet minister calculating ever so briefly his appropriate spin, or from ordinary citizens genuinely perplexed by the moral or political ambiguities of the questions suddenly tossed their way.

In contrast to his previous book, *Leaving Japan*, a critical Parthian shot at a society he found too narrow-minded to hold him, *Jihad in Paradise* is Millard's paean to the multiethnic pluralism and tolerance he has come to savor in his new home in Southeast Asia, a book brimming with his love for the region and its peoples with their diversity as warm and lush as the lands in which they live. It is above all, however, the author's alarm bell as to how all this is placed in jeopardy by the rise of radical Islamism with its instrument of terror and its goal of a region-wide theocratic state.

Too long have Americans and others worried by the rise of

militant Islamism—and hoping for the emergence of a moderate, modern-minded, Islamic counterforce—focused their attention on the "failed states" in the western half of that great arc of Muslim societies stretching from Morocco to Indonesia, while ignoring the successes in the eastern sector. These include effective secularist integration in India and Bangladesh, but especially the more tolerant forms of Islam long practiced in Southeast Asia, where they continue to draw strength from economies vastly more advanced, and from political regimes far more open and democratic than those of North Africa and the Middle East. In West Asia, the likes of al Qaeda threaten to abort modernist development as yet unborn. In East Asia, the likes of Jemaah Islamiyah threaten to tear down promising structures already in place.

To revamp and reverse the old adage about New York: If moderate Islam can't make it in the Lion City and Kuala Lumpur, it won't make it anywhere. Millard zeroes in on these two "straits" states because he knows them best, and because Chinese-dominated Singapore and Muslim-majority Malaysia stand on the threatened cusp of that more cosmopolitan Islam on which the West has set its hopes. Millard's "paradise" is tripartite—physical, economic, and sociocultural. If the Eden of the travel brochures came unstuck with the terrorist attack on Bali's tourist idyll, radical Islamism threatens to undermine the key integrating force of widening affluence and equal economic opportunity with terror-driven destabilization and theologically driven economic prescriptions. But if racial and religious accommodation breaks down, then paradise is lost forever—so it is to the chances for that particular disaster that Millard addresses the central question of his book.

To what extent have the rise of radical Islamism, terrorist actions in the immediate region, and more distant events like 9/11 or the American invasions of Iraq and Afghanistan led—or threatened to lead—the Muslim communities of Singapore and Malaysia to shift their primary identity and loyalty from citizenship in their local multicultural states to membership in a transnational, religiously defined, pan-Islamic agenda? To sort out the emotional, intellectual, and political responses to that question from Muslims and their non-Muslim neighbors alike, Millard takes his readers into homes, offices, and coffee shops for a fast-paced, lapidary string of conversations with university pundits, fellow journalists, government officials, lawyers for terrorist suspects, absconding dissidents, once-banned female authors, and political leaders at all levels, including Singapore founding father Lee Kuan Yew and Kelantan chief minister Nik Aziz, who personify the two alternatives—multiethnic versus Islamist—now at hand.

While drawing on recent scholarly expertise for context, this is not an academic text. Nor is it one of those potboilers by roving journalists who swoop in for a quick kill after the event—a genre we shall see plenty of if and when regional terrorist outrages and radical Islamist ideological fervor pass the critical mark. Millard, rather, is a resident, capable of weaving his story from the bottom up as well as top down, who gives us a just-in-time warning before rather than after things get worse.

From his local sources, including the government's white paper probing the psychology of its Jemaah Islamiyah detainees, arrested after their aborted plot against Western embassies, Millard concludes that, in Singapore at least, the attraction of the Muslim community to radical Islamism is for the moment minimal. The arrested terrorists seem driven to murderous extremes not at all by local conditions, but by a variety of personal pathologies ending up in a death cult. Indeed, one of the two major subthemes of this book is an upbeat report card on Singapore's government-imposed experiment toward an authentically multicultural society, moving beyond mere passive tolerance to an active mutual appreciation and a rich layering of joint civic interaction—all yet to be achieved—that will seal off the drains of Muslim alienation and separatism permanently.

The other subtheme, like a ground bass to Millard's entire story, are the questions most frequently asked of Singapore by the West. When, if ever, will the "soft authoritarianism" adopted for the sake of rapid economic growth with social stability give way, as in South Korea and Taiwan, to a genuine liberal democracy? Has the indisputable good of ethnic harmony been bought at too high a cost on another good, that of personal freedom?

My own recent visits to Singapore bear out the general judgment of this book that wide areas once taboo in the arts and social behavior such as frontal nudity in the movies, marital hanky-panky, homosexuality, and the merits of a bohemian lifestyle—all unthinkable a mere decade or so ago—have now been opened to public discussion. Race, religion, and criticism of the government remain under wraps—an enormous tent, to be sure. Millard, who knows Japan well from his eleven years there as a journalist, notes the striking similarity of Japanese and Singaporean bureaucrats in publicly calling for more "creativity" and "individuality" while remaining scared stiff of having things get out of control should they actually loosen the tether.

Singapore's chief impetus for political liberalization now comes from the need for imaginative private-sector leadership to move the country, with no time to lose, from a manufacturing to a knowledge-driven economy. Entrepreneurship, innovation, and risk taking are the mantras of the day; and Singapore Management University has even made the study of creative thinking a core university subject, compulsory for all students no matter what their field of interest. To move beyond the oxymorons of "managed creativity" and "managed openness," however, the new rank of innovators will have to be given freedom of expression—including, it seems to me, an eventual lifting of political censorship—and the opportunity to make mistakes without being punished for them. When the yoke of bureaucratic authority chafes, however, the Singaporeans at least have the saving grace of knowing when they are being had, and the ability to laugh about it in private—far more, in my experience, than do the Japanese. And to that extent they are considerably closer to the liberal and individualistic world of the West.

Millard moved from Tokyo to Singapore with his Japanese wife four years ago in order to remove their now-ten-year-old Eurasian son from the potential bullying of racially different children in Japanese schools. Not surprisingly, he brings a very personal note to his salute to Singapore's multicultural achievement, together with an open rebuke to Japan's cultural and racial insularism. The absence of those traits, he argues, gives the island city-state a significant jump on Japan in its potential for creative self-reform. However, he wryly admits that the Japanese, with so much cash stashed away, have been able to tread water on economic rejuvenation for a whole decade—a luxury that would sink Singapore in short order.

One thought-provoking insight tucked away by implication in this little book is an early test at the local, gut-reaction, level of Samuel Huntington's speculation in *The Clash of Civilizations* that the Islamic and Confucian worlds eventually might gang up on the West. Although Huntington's monitory delineation of civilizational fissures is as timely as Millard's book, and any number of constellations in the interstate arena are conceivable over the long run, on page after page, *Jihad in Paradise* contrasts the impractical rigidities and reckless fantasies of the radical Islamist world view with the concrete, pragmatic, politically cautious, and economically vigorous mind of the modern-world Singaporean Chinese.

As this marvelously readable author puts it: "It should be tended like a prize garden."

Ivan Hall
Chiang Mai, Thailand
September 2003

Acknowledgments

There were numerous people who contributed to this book, and without whom, in fact, it could not have been written. I would like to thank a few of them. First, Professor Kirpal Singh of Singapore Management University introduced me to many of the people who were interviewed and who shared their knowledge so generously. Second, Mike Hall patiently put up with a verbal stream of ideas for more than a year, then had the good grace to read a rough manuscript even as he was packing to move to Australia. Nabeel Mohideen in New Delhi offered valuable guidance and insight. Shamim Adam provided a constant source of information. Ivan Hall kept me focused on the task at hand, and Ron Lloyd provided perspective on world events with e-mails from snowy northern Idaho. Professor Pang Eng Fong of Singapore Management University brought statistical and developmental aspects of Singapore into clearer focus after reading a later draft. Professor Farid Alatas of National University of Singapore also read a later draft and advised me on the results of my research into recent Islamic history and Wahhabism. The support that I received in writing this book was excellent and crucial. Any errors or mistakes in judgment on these pages, therefore, are mine alone.

INTRODUCTION

Singapore, Bali, Kuala Lumpur, Jakarta, Manila . . . the names vibrated exotically. And there was more. In the mid-1990s, these places were safe, for the most part prosperous, and located in one of the most promising regions on earth. Southeast Asia burgeoned with economic growth and growing political stability. The Japanese miracle was replicating itself through smaller, aggressive "tiger economies" that expanded by exporting manufactured goods to Western markets, creating wealth, and raising the standards of living enjoyed by their peoples. Things had never been better.

Then life demonstrated how things can change for the worse. By the first years of the new century, only Singapore and Malaysia displayed much residual economic strength after the Asian financial crisis of 1997–98; a global downturn in the electronics and computer industry after America's dot-com bust; and attacks by Islamist militants who were essentially brigades of a worldwide assault upon the West—on its systems of commerce, and on modernity itself that had found its most iconic expression in the suicide crashes into the World Trade Center on September 11, 2001.

Tiny, well-governed Singapore, with its educated, well-paid workforce, endured recession and two roundups of homegrown terrorists, as well as a deadly viral outbreak, yet forged ahead by increasingly diversifying an agile economy from shipping, manufacturing, and petrochemicals to making and testing semiconductors and electronic components to researching and producing pharmaceuticals and chemicals. It liberalized its financial industry, expanded telecommunications regionally and moved into cutting-edge biotechnical research. Malaysia, where Islamic governments ruled two states, was less successful on a per capita basis, although Prime Minister Mahathir Mohamad kept extremists at bay and the economy moving with a unique ability to conduct the contending political forces of his nation as if they were his own personal orchestra. It will be difficult for his successor, Abdullah Ahmad Badawi, to equal such a political maestro.

Indonesia and the Philippines, less-developed countries that had long suffered under corrupt governments and injustice, where average incomes had been low and infant mortality rates high in the best of times, were more receptive to the message of Islamist militancy, and each harbored groups that were willing to kill innocents to bring about a Southeast Asian Islamist state. This, they referred to as their jihad, their effort to fulfill what they were assured by their religious leaders was God's will. There was a sense that popular revolutions might be possible, something akin to the one that Ayatollah Khomeini rode to power in Iran. In countries where governments are weak and corrupt and people cannot feed their families properly, revolutionary ideas have always found fertile ground, if only to provide scraps of hope to those who have none. An insurrection against a government under the banner of Islam was no different, except that it had an inherent spiritual justification so that none had to be manufactured in the way a "divine emperor" was created as a useful tool by the governing elites during Japan's Meiji period. Islamists, united in a cause of violent political insurrection, are already the truest of believers, have submitted their wills to the preachers who claim to represent God, and are sometimes prepared even for suicide in the cause of their leaders' political ambitions.

The unification of Southeast Asia into an Islamist state is fairly grandiose, as such ambitions go, and it became clear in late 2001 that there were hundreds of Islamists throughout the region willing to slay infidels, which for them included even Muslims who did not agree with their aims. Members of the Indonesia-based Jemaah Islamiyah and Abu Saayaf of the Philippines had received training from al Qaeda in Afghanistan and were moving around the region with several tons of explosives.

Gleaming, first-world Singapore, with its upwardly mobile citizens and meritocracy was dwarfed beside hulking Indonesia, its corrupt post-Suharto elites and 220 million people, most of them poor Muslims with little education, except for the more prosperous Hindu Balinese with their flourishing tourist industry and some primitive animists scattered through the tropical forests of the more remote islands. The Philippines had slumped after several years of moderate post-Marcos economic growth, and Islamist insurrections were flaring in its southern islands.

Most of these developments were unexpected in the late 1990s when I moved my family from Japan to Singapore so we could live in a multiethnic society and my son could attend the island's excellent primary school system. One of the annual holiday events in his school was Ethnic Harmony Day, for which the principal asked students not to wear the clothing of their own people but, rather, to don the traditional garb of another ethnic group so that they could feel the other's identity, if only in a superficial way. Teaching children to understand other races and religions seemed sane and hopeful. The attacks and bombings since have done nothing to alter that. While violence may have occurred that was less than sane and not at all hopeful, it is important to recall what went before, and what in time will come again if people do not give in to the zealots who wish to deepen racial, ethnic, and religious divisions that run like shadowy fault lines through humanity.

Two points should be made here: First, this is not an "inside Singapore" story seeking to reveal the fine detail and nuances of the city-state. That is best left to local writers who know them far better than I. And, second, while fortunate enough to live in Singapore for a number of years and travel in Southeast Asia, I am neither native to the region nor an expert by virtue of years of study. Like all international journalists I am an outsider, if a deeply interested one, immersed in the story of the place and times with its particular human realities, while attempting also to comprehend its regional and global dimensions.

That story follows.

Jihad in Paradise

ARRIVAL AND DISCOVERY

1999—SINGAPORE IS A SPLENDID TROPICAL ISLAND. It's not the natural sort like Tahiti, but is rather more unusual—a highly developed economy set in an equatorial region. If you are a romantic sort who conceives of reality as an out-of-reach ideal to which the world consistently fails to measure up, then for a number of reasons that we will look at later, you may find Singapore to be unsatisfactory. If you realistically compare the workaday aspects of cities and nations, however, you may feel differently. In a comparative light, Singapore emerges as a lovely environment in which to live, work, and raise your children.

My son, Emerson, was born in Japan, where he went to a Buddhist kindergarten and spoke Japanese with his friends and of course with his Japanese mother. When he reached the age of five, we began to worry about putting him in local schools. The American school was far across Tokyo and tuition was roughly what you would pay to send your child to Harvard. Japanese public schools were notorious for *ijime*, bullying of anyone who did not conform to strict norms of behavior and appearance, and our son was not Japanese but a beautiful Eurasian child.

My news agency sent me to Singapore for some training, and our future appeared in the local newspaper: A first-section picture displayed a row of smiling primary-school children who had made high scores on their exams. Some appeared to be ethnically Chinese or East Asian, while others may have been Indian or Malay. And indeed, Singapore was alive with people of various races and mixtures mingling easily, quite unlike the harsh spirit of racial purity prevalent in Japan. Singaporeans are roughly 75 percent ethnically Chinese, 15 percent Malay, and 6 percent Indian, with intermarriages increasingly common.

Still, the situation was better than Japan only in a relative sense. There were deeply felt problems in Singapore, too. The indigenous Malay-Muslims have a generally lower educational level than the more recently arrived ethnic Chinese or Indian segments of the population, and smaller average incomes as well, although they do much better than their brethren across the channel in Malaysia. Still, as one scholar put it, if a Malay-Muslim should "venture to start a business of his own, not only does he lack the international contacts Chinese and Indian commerce has established for centuries, but he has to face the active opposition of those sojourners in his native land."[1] As in other multiethnic societies scattered across the face of the earth, prejudices arise all too naturally.

Prejudice is at least partially a by-product of a categorizing aspect of our minds that is necessary, but that may also have harmful effects if we are not aware of its processes. Those who study the shimmering phenomena of our mental lives say that we all must categorize because it enables us to operate efficiently with assumptions that are fairly accurate. We cannot question each fact relating to our lives every minute, or, like so many emotionally paralyzed Hamlets, we would have time for little else. We generalize and classify and get on with life, but our categorical modes of thought can go factually and morally wrong when we apply them to people. We can assign each race, ethnic group, or religion characteristics as a sociological shorthand that catches them in our categorical nets, but fails to realize each person is singular, an individual collection of experiences and values rising up as a unique wave from an ocean of humanity.

If your ears are open to casual conversations and jokes around Singapore, you may hear that Chinese think only of money, that Malays have little ambition, and that Indians are duplicitous, while Caucasians are decadent imperialists. Generalities of this sort bear little relationship to reality, and they feed fantasies that arise when we lack motivation to understand individuals, fantasies often born from unconscious fears and desires that may even be transformed into aggression. Freud wrote that "closely related races keep one another at arm's length; the South German cannot endure the North German, the Englishman casts every kind of aspersion upon the Scot, the Spaniard despises the Portuguese. We are no longer astonished that greater differences should lead to an almost insuperable repugnance, such as the Gallic people feel for the German, the Aryan for the Semite, the white races for the colored."[2] Our tribal prejudices, it seems, have been with us for a long time, probably since Neolithic humans banded into hunting packs to contest for food and territory. A question of the highest priority, as we try to form multiethnic societies and move fitfully toward a functioning pluralism that will be necessary for the global society that seems to be our inescapable collective fate, is how can we first deal with the effects of prejudice, and some day, perhaps, prevent prejudice from arising at all?

Malay-Muslims are indigenous to the Indonesian archipelago as well as to the Malaysian Peninsula, including Singapore, and for the most part passed from primitive animistic beliefs through Hinduism to Islam during the last millennium. By around 1400, Islam predominated throughout the area with the exception of Hindu Bali and some remote tribes that clung to older traditions such as shamanism. Malays in a developmental context, however, have lagged behind Chinese and Indian immigrants who have taken up residence in the region and often engaged in commerce. One reason for this may be the Malays' "failure to specialize and a failure to acquire and realize the importance of capital,"[3] we are told by scholar Richard Winstedt, writing around mid-century. Perhaps culture does matter, and the Malays are striving to close a gap that has existed for some time. Winstedt argued that the lack of specialization stemmed from the small Malay *kampung* villages, which of necessity produced generalists, and because the bountiful nature of the land made living relatively easy. The scholar Pang Eng Fong wrote in a similar vein that the traditional Malay social system of the villages emphasized community spirit and personal contentment, and that parents "paid more attention to the inculcation of social and religious values than to the values of competition and material pursuits."[4] Winstedt added that the "prime difficulty of the Malay today is how to acquire capital to apply to industry. If he wants to enter commerce, he finds that Chinese and Indians reserve employment for their own races."[5] Such exclusionary policies create the problem of finding "an entry into commerce for the Malay, without which his race must feel more and more discontent and resentment."[6] This problem does not seem to have faded completely away in the interim five decades since it was noted, although Singapore has tried in various ways to address it.

A more contemporary scholar, Lily Zubaidah Rahim, argues that the long life of the "culture deficit thesis" is in fact partially responsible for the situation in which Malays find themselves in Singapore, which she sees as one in which they are discriminated against by ethnic Chinese employers who may well believe that Malays will always trail behind the rest of Singaporean society. Thus, "like a self-fulfilling prophecy, the dominant understanding of the Malay marginality that is informed by the cultural deficit . . . may well prove to be a major contributor to the persisting socio-economic and educational marginality of the Malay community."[7] While there may seem to be some circularity inherent in her argument, there is probably also substance. Employers may overlook qualified, ambitious Malay applicants for jobs because of their acceptance of timeworn assumptions that ultimately amount to nothing more than discriminatory prejudices.

Singapore's primary-school students scored highest in the world in science and mathematics tests, research showed, because its educational system was rigorous and demanding.

There was a good reason for that. Singapore is a tiny island, roughly the size of Chicago, with no resources except its people, so it has worked hard to develop them.

Singapore is what the scholar Chalmers Johnson termed a capitalist developmental state, originally to explain how Japan's rapid growth differed from that of both Western free-market and Soviet command-style economies. The term was later applied to other Asian states, including Korea, Taiwan, and Singapore, which emulated Japan's export-based approach and its phenomenal success to varying degrees. Singapore, however, did not defend its home market from exports as did Japan, and it opted for education in the English language, which are important differences. Still, these were all late-developing economies that attained growth quickly through government participation that included industrial planning; encouraging high savings rates; funneling capital to chosen industries; and, in Singapore's case, government establishment and ownership of banks, airlines, ports, telecommunications, and a key holding company that accounts for about 20 percent of its stock market. Another crucial component of the strategy is solid infrastructure, which includes excellent mass education to create a trained workforce, something that Singapore has done as well as any country in the world.

A nation for fewer than four decades, Singapore's 3 million citizens enjoyed an annual per capita income of more than $21,000, nearly every resident family owned its home, and the infant mortality rate—so painfully high in nearby countries such as Indonesia where forty-one children out of every thousand die—was among the lowest in the world at 3.6, better than most Scandinavian countries, and much better than the

United States, where 6.7 children die and the rate for black children is twice as high. If you want your heart broken, take some time to observe the misery of children in Asia's slums, a sorry predicament to which Singapore offers a brilliant exception. What could be a more important characteristic of a good society than how few of its children it allows to die, and how well it nurtures them?

While the capitalist developmental approach has increased the incomes of Singaporeans ten times over, the price they paid—in addition to hard work—was the suppression of some political and media freedoms in order to maintain a social discipline that has allowed them to focus almost entirely on expanding their economy. The city-state's newspapers facilitate the needs of the state rather than criticize it, as "editors are expected to have an instinctive grasp of Singapore's national interests and how to protect them."[8] The Religious Harmony Act makes derogatory statements about the island's various religions illegal. And there is a rather ambiguous set of what are called "out of bounds markers," which allow for criticism of government policies, but not direct attacks on officials or calling into question their fitness to govern.[9]

The originator of the developmental model, Japan, is unique in that it continues to maintain social cohesion through a quasi-religious devotion of employees to their companies and of the media to the needs of a soft authoritarian state, a situation that has for centuries been culturally and psychologically inculcated. In Korea and Taiwan, many of the suppressed liberties have in recent years been allowed. In Singapore, this has not yet happened, and still, for several reasons I feel no urge to be overtly critical. First, writers from Ian Buruma on the left to William Safire on the right have already applied themselves so completely to condemnation that there is no sense in reiterating their work, which has left unexamined for too long another side of this case on which some well-deserved light should be shined. Second, as we will see, Singapore in recent years has begun instituting a piecemeal liberalization policy. And third, some patience might be in order, because the democratizing process seems to be more a matter of correct timing than of permanent refusal, which we will also explore. While there is lively debate among Singaporeans in private about their constrained political avenues of expression, the city's not-so-distant past as a poor nation, and the disturbing example of Indonesia, with its millions able to vote freely while living amid abject poverty and corruption, help prevent any eruptions of significant social dissonance among Singaporeans.

The government's legitimacy is rooted deeply in its superior economic performance and its abstinence from corruption—it is rated best in Asia by watchdog groups like Transparency International. Singaporeans are satisfied enough for the time being to count their blessings. The fact is, things are good. The developmental model may offer the best chance for a poor country to achieve the kind of economic success that allows not just its elites, but its broad citizenry, to flourish. What permutations may follow the developmental phase, however, are for the most part unknown, because it is only now that they are being explored. The catch-up decades are coming to an end. The island is currently embarked on a transformation project to "remake Singapore," in which it is trying to introduce a stronger spirit of creativity and entrepreneurship among its students as a component of their educations. The chances are that where such rigorous universal education ventures, an expanding middle class and enhanced liberty will eventually follow. The civic and economic responsibilities flowing from those freedoms, however, will be complex and heavy, Singaporeans are bound to discover.

Singapore is the greenest of cities. Soaring blocks of modern flats and low rows of shophouses from the colonial era are integrated with jungle groves, over which mossy trunks and branches hold aloft leafy canopies. The island is a rainforest that has been partially settled and developed, a fact of which its verdant, blossoming swathes serve to remind. More than half a million trees line the byways and rise from grassy spaces, many of them native and others transplants that have found a friendly soil and climate. Many of the more than 100 species have been planted over the past three decades through a government program. Others date from colonial times, including the shady South American raintrees that spread like graceful towers, tangled with vines and splashed with staghorns and birdnest ferns that burst light-green from the crooks of dark mossy limbs. At lower heights are coral trees with orange blooms, the banyan with its multiple roots, and types of ficus. There is a variety of palms that hold out luminescent fronds to catch the sun, strange tropical fruits, and blooming from low bushes and vines are the flowers, bougainvillea, jasmine, orchids of all sizes and colors, fragrant gardenias, water lilies, and sacred lotus. It is an island of luxuriant greenery and flowers.

This is a remarkable accomplishment in light of a skyscraping financial district, one of the world's most efficient airports and busiest container-shipping ports. Half the island remains in a natural state or has been replanted. The father of modern Singapore, Senior Minister Lee Kuan Yew, once said, "I have always believed that a blighted urban landscape, a concrete jungle, destroys the human spirit. We need the greenery of nature to lift our spirits."[10]

The forests may no longer be prowled by tigers, except those found on the labels of the local brew, Tiger Beer; but legend has it that one was shot during the late colonial period in a bar at the elegant Raffles Hotel, whose rooms were once favored by the writer Somerset Maugham and the actor Noel Coward, and where it is said the Singapore Sling was invented to serve the sturdy, red-faced British adventurers who are no longer masters of Singapore, having been driven from Asia along with the Dutch and other colonial powers by the Japanese in 1941.

A colleague from Pakistan, upon visiting Singapore for the first time remarked that he was a bit nervous at the "lack of human problems" he observed as we walked along a sidewalk crowded with well-dressed workers and fashionable women, past a walled Chinese temple and along a shady boulevard toward an old waterfront lined with gentrified restaurants and bistros. Having traveled through the northern part of India and having observed the misery that residents of that part of the world must endure, his view was not difficult to understand. Adjacent to the almost unearthly beauty of the Taj Mahal, ghastly cripples beg for money, many of them purposely misshapen as babies by their parents so they will have a vocation and enough to eat.

It is that sort of horror from which Singapore has been saved. You may enjoy a conversation over lunch in a palm-lined courtyard, glass-covered and air-conditioned, or along a shaded riverside, and when a workday is finished you can call a taxi and within minutes be wherever you make your home. During a decade in Tokyo, I had never become accustomed to the city's drab sprawl or to the three hours each day on lurching trains crowded with grim and often drunk salarymen. The fabric of daily life in Singapore was of a significantly higher quality. Singaporeans often eat their dinners at outdoor hawker centers, or at bistros by the river or the seacoast. Outdoor dining is popular because evenings are cooler than the torrid heat of the day, and the food on offer ranges from local specialties such as chili crab to regional dishes like coconut-flavored laksa to a full variety of curries to the marinated meat dishes of the northern frontier of the Indian subcontinent to European or Chinese fine dining. The spectrum of food is remarkable, and Singaporeans debate constantly about new restaurants and where the best versions of certain dishes may be found.

Singaporean writer Kishore Mahbubani, who has served as the island's envoy to the United Nations, spoke effusively about the attractions of the city-state for families, keeping in mind that there are about one million foreigners living there.

"Yes, it's good for families," Mahbubani said. "There is empirical evidence. Foreign diplomats love to come and stay in Singapore. It's safe. Children and women can go around on their own. It has an excellent educational system. For those who want to enjoy family life, Singapore is a great place to live. Also, the variety of food is one of the main attractions. Unlike Hong Kong, where you get mainly Chinese food, in Singapore you get all kinds of Asian dishes."

What had enabled Singapore to develop so far in less than four decades? I asked.

Mahbubani's short answer was leadership and luck. "We've had exceptionally good leadership, especially the first generation, including Lee Kuan Yew. And he had a first-rate team. Then we've had peaceful leadership transitions into equally competent teams. The policies of good governance have been remarkable."

How had Singapore managed to foster smooth ethnic relations since the country was born amid Chinese-Malay racial riots in the mid-1960s?

"The first thing was the fact that the government was extremely fair, along with being strict. Then there are four official languages, and as you know, in many countries minorities are not allowed to use their languages. In Singapore they are encouraged to do so. The principle of meritocracy in government also means that there is no discrimination. I have cousins who have grown up in other former British colonies, like Sri Lanka, and you see how things are down there. Singapore has also avoided ethnic enclaves, which can generate a lot of anger. When you have people living side by side their relations can be closer."

There were no ghettos on the island, no desperately poor ethnic communities, and for that alone Singapore might be studied in Western nations and emulated at least to a degree that does not conflict with the liberties those nations have achieved.

The most attractive aspect of Singapore for us, however, more than the orchids that grew everywhere, more than the brilliantly colored birds that sang in the trees outside our windows, was the primary-school system. Emerson turned six just after we arrived and spoke Japanese as a first language. I was the only English-speaker he knew, so his skills with it were little better than my Japanese. We communicated through a language of expressions, gestures, and phrases that links fathers and sons. Upon arrival, we moved into a two-story terrace house in a village-style arrangement with a shared swimming pool and common green, which was a great relief after years of cramped tatami-room apartments in Japan. On his first day of primary one, we took pictures of Emerson waiting for the bus, so small and thin, wearing the blue shorts and white shirt of his school, lugging heavy texts and workbooks in a backpack. I hoped that we had done the right thing in leaving Japan.

The first week, he began returning with homework, which has continued unabated. I was delighted. Singapore schools have English as a basic language, and all students must learn a second as well, usually Mandarin, Bahasa Malaysia, or Tamil. Emerson focused on English, with some remedial training the school provided on Saturdays, and within six months he was speaking rather fluently, if with a Singaporean accent. He had also acquired an ethnically varied group of buddies, ranging from Australian to Chinese to Indian to Bangladeshi to Thai to Malay. Later, we put him in an after-hours class to learn to read and write Japanese, and he also began to study martial arts and move steadily up the rankings in his taekwondo group. In less than a year, Emerson went from being shy and uncommunicative to rather outgoing, even brash and humorous. He flourished like a transplanted sapling in rich soil.

Western expatriates sometimes complain that Singapore is a little on the quiet side, that it has a sterile and controlled environment that is too clean and well-planned to be "authentically" Asian. And while it is true that there is no sprawling bar district like Kabukicho in Tokyo, nothing resembling Pattaya Beach in Thailand, Singapore has some nice bistros. It also has one of the best zoos in the world, a lovely bird park, and a gorgeous orchid garden. It is a garden city of traditional cultures in which children are valued for themselves, and are nurtured as resources to ensure the island's economic and political future. It has always been clear that Singapore will succeed or fail according to the efforts of its people. The diverse ethnic groups have little choice but to struggle to educate themselves and rise together, which they have done to an admirable degree. Singapore is a successful nation in which organized striving has created an exemplary capitalist economy. It had a solid game plan and followed it, and is now trying hard to learn to improvise after being presented with a shifting global reality that demands it.

After two years of living and working in the city-state, Singapore didn't seem to be the kind of place where fanatical terrorists would be concealing themselves among their own people, laying deadly plans, silently waiting to receive orders from Middle Eastern Islamist commanders in Afghanistan to wreak havoc on their nation, on their people and economy. But Afghanistan had become a "campground from which an Arab army was battling America,"[11] and Singapore was a developed and open nation, bristling with American and European interests, a finance center, a manufacturing enclave, and the most Westernized nation in Southeast Asia. This meant Singapore was also a desirable recruiting ground for terrorists who despised modernity, as well as their primary target in the region for destruction.

Questions arose like startled birds: What sort of people

could kill their fellow citizens, others of their own faith, and innocents from foreign countries, and do it in the name of religion, a spiritual condition in which compassion is said to be a central quality, in which humans are usually elevated to feel some common identity with others? Why would such people wish to commit mass murders when they were living comfortable lives within the embrace of a prosperous society? And what had caused such a descent into madness? It was important to form some understanding of this gathering threat, where it had originated, why it murdered, and how it sought to slay even more. While Singapore may be geographically distant from the terrorism of September 11, it remains part of ground zero of a global jihad, coveted as part of a Southeast Asian Islamist state conceived in the same minds that respond to an ideology whose most prominent features are terrorism and death.

SOURCES OF JIHAD

2001—WE BEGAN TO EXPLORE SOUTHEAST ASIA, SNORKELING IN THE CRYSTAL WATERS OFF MALAYSIAN ISLANDS WHERE MULTICOL- ORED FISH DARTED AND DANCED AROUND CORAL REEFS, ENJOYING THE PLEASANT BEACH RESORTS OF THAILAND AND SIGHING AT THE TRANSCENDENT SPLENDOR OF BALINESE TEMPLE DANCERS AND THEIR GRACEFUL, DISCIPLINED EXPRESSIONS OF HINDU MYTHOLOGY ON WARM TROPICAL NIGHTS BEFORE THE UPRAISED GATES OF VINE- ENCRUSTED STONE TEMPLES.

The Asian financial crisis was nearing an end and com- merce in the region was again starting to percolate, with the exception of Indonesia, which began to look like a basket case amid the corruption and debt of its post-Suharto era. Then the dot-com bubble burst and economies—including Singapore's—with dependencies on the U.S. computer market slumped again, all helping to make 2001 vastly different than we might have imagined. Not that it was any comfort, but others, including the late filmmaker Stanley Kubrick and eminent science fiction writer Arthur C. Clarke had also gotten 2001 wrong. It was no space odyssey. While an enigmatic and puzzling message was indeed addressed to humanity, it came from a source somewhat closer to home, if no less strange, than the dark side of the moon. It was delivered from the mountains of Afghanistan, via four hijacked jetliners. Perhaps the scholar Samuel Huntington had shown a more realistic understanding of humanity and our times with his foreboding vision of dangerous fault lines threatening to develop between humanity's cultures: "Wars between clans, tribes, ethnic groups, religious communities, and nations have been prevalent in every era and in every civilization because they are rooted in the identities of peoples. . . . They also tend to be vicious and bloody, since fundamental issues of identity are at stake."[1]

The Japanese showed how stubbornly a culture could cling to values that no longer served it, especially when its political elites feared change so desperately that they kept society underfoot and restrained by an iron chain of tradition that passed down through the generations. Singapore, on the other hand, was a fledgling nation that had jettisoned much of its time-worn baggage for the sake of an efficient economy. The island's experiment in nation building was fascinating, and the primary-school system excellent, so a return to the United States had been put off to some vague future when a friend called one evening and said that an airplane had flown into the World Trade Center. I turned on the television and watched as a second jetliner and fiery hell descended over New York.

The twin towers crumbled into surreal billowing smoke and dust that made a war zone of Manhattan.

In retrospect, considering a series of horrific events that included the Jonestown Christian cult deaths, the Waco conflagration, and the quiet Heaven's Gate suicides among others, the September 11 attacks probably should not have been so unexpected. There was an irrational impulse at large in the world. In the wake of swift technological and cultural changes came loss, alienation, and a threatening despair. This was sometimes compounded by poverty and indignation at the injustice of corrupt governments. People whose identities were bound up in traditional religions recoiled in fear at what they perceived as a spiritual wasteland. They sometimes sought answers and salvation from those claiming to offer them, including cult leaders and militant Islamist clerics. When subsequently gripped by overpowering "religious" urges, the faithful, the believers, could be moved to commit acts of purest evil, to kill themselves, and to slay others. The scholar of religions, Karen Armstrong, wrote that "the modernizing process can induce great anxiety. As their world changes, people feel disoriented and lost. . . . They can experience a numbing loss of identity and a paralyzing despair. The most common emotions are helplessness and a fear of annihilation that can, in extreme circumstances, erupt in violence."[2] Such extreme circumstances, it seems, are upon us in these times, to the extent that hatred, rage, and violence are becoming quite commonplace.

Soon after the fall of the twin towers, my news agency's Singapore office began serving as a conduit for stories from Pakistan—a nation of scant economic vitality that had previously supplied only a trickle of mostly agricultural business news—and from Afghanistan, a dysfunctional, war-shattered country that lacked a stock exchange and barely had a central bank. Our quiet outpost grew into a major artery for a flood of information pumped from a temporary heart, because people worldwide suddenly wished to know more about the ethnic groups and tribes of the subcontinent's frontier, their peculiar systems of barter and finance, and their strange cruelties. These bearded men of al Qaeda seemed possessed with a mad desire to kill innocent people. Who were they? What hatred drove them? These questions and a thousand others occurred in those first weeks, allowing no peace even in dreams, where they played out wicked themes of death and inhumanity, costumed by settings of other times and places. One fact emerged early: There were ideological linkages from Islamist extremists in Afghanistan and Pakistan back to their origins in Saudi Arabia and Egypt. There were connections to Kashmir, Indonesia, Malaysia, and the Philippines. The thought occurred: Could this be an Islamist theocracy breaking away with a billion people, most of the world's oil and nuclear weapons, following a heretofore obscure terrorist named Osama bin Laden? It was a chilling scenario, less rational, and so potentially as dangerous as the Soviet Union during the cold war.

The first chaotic weeks after the attacks, so fraught with psychological urgency, were also a time of a strange unity for Americans, even those of us overseas. As alternately horrifying and inspiring images flickered across our television screens and illustrated the emergence of a new threat to our way of life, it was also clear that victims of the hijackers were of all races and religions, as were the rescue workers, emergency medical people, and journalists bringing us stories.

At such a time of heightened awareness, prejudice had no place. We were equally under threat from a fanatical adversary that had driven us to function together with no questions asked. If only for a brief period, we participated in a unified America. A psychologist interviewed on television also observed this phenomenon and remarked how unfortunate it was that a tragedy had been required to bring the country together. Perhaps this was true, but mingling with my horror and fear, I felt strands of joy. For a few tense weeks, Americans did indeed hold certain truths to be self-evident. Perhaps we will never again feel quite so fragmented.

I sat riveted to television news late into each night—which was early morning in New York and Washington—and scoured the Internet for information, gleaning scraps of meaning wherever they could be found in an attempt to absorb a confusing new reality. I asked a Muslim woman, a reporter at my company, to lunch so that we could discuss the events that were unfolding. Shamim was a third-generation Singaporean of Indian ethnicity with a warm, radiant smile and a generous personality that I instinctively liked. Each day at work she wore the traditional *tudung* covering her head and flowing down to her loose robes. With a journalism degree from an Australian university, Shamim was a hard-working and ambitious reporter, a keen observer of Singapore's business and political scene, as well as president of a Manchester United fan club. There was a multiplicity of forces at play within her. We entered a busy Southeast Asian–style food court and found seats at a table while other workers on lunch break streamed through in search of tasty bowls of noodles, chicken rice, duck, seafood, sandwiches, sushi, curry, nearly anything, it seemed. Much of it was *halal* or acceptable to Islamic dietary practices. I asked Shamim what local Muslims were making of Osama bin Laden.

Some of the more fundamentalist people she knew were uncertain about bin Laden, she said, and a few even wondered whether he might be the Hidden Imam, something like a savior in Christian theology or Jewish prophecy. I recalled televised images of a tall, slender, bearded man in flowing white robes, smiling softly and appearing Christ-like were he not squeezing off rounds from an assault rifle. Was this a person who inspired humanity to realize its divine potential? Was there some obscure way in which the attack on the World Trade Center could be seen as a moral act?

"No," she said, softly, "It wasn't right. Those who died there were innocent. But still, some people are wondering if Osama might not be the one."

There was another level of conflict, a propaganda war, raging across the world's airwaves and television screens. Bin Laden had "produced a piece of high political theater that he hoped would reach the audience that concerned him most: the *umma*, or universal Islamic community."[3] It was only natural that there would be some among the believers who were afraid to make a wrong choice, or any choice, in case truth eventually revealed itself in some mysterious way they had not anticipated. It was an unsettling notion.

"Innocent people, all dead," I repeated, to myself as much as to Shamim.

"Yes, they were innocent," she said, a shadow falling over her brow and her shining eyes.

I had no wish to push her on this point. She was young, but capable of realism and making her own way through public images and spin to the essence of things. Shamim devoted private time to tutoring children and had herself been a student of Mendaki, a Muslim self-help organization established two decades earlier to improve the social and economic standing of the Malay-Muslim community. Its logo was a blue globe emblazoned with an Arabic word for "read," the first word revealed by Allah to the Prophet.

Days later, the island's highest Islamic authority, the mufti, called for Muslims and all Singaporeans to continue living in harmony even if the United States attacked bin Laden's al Qaeda followers and the Taliban rulers of Afghanistan.[4] A Muslim group, the Singapore National Front, called on the government to "act swiftly and decisively against any group that tries to instill suspicions and hatred that could disrupt racial harmony among Singaporeans of different races and religions."[5] Singaporeans were accustomed to swimming in a sea of multiethnicity with a sort of studied grace. They had learned to mix races and religions more artfully than peoples of most countries, including the Western ones, where separation was the norm, discrimination all too common, and riots erupted sporadically.

In mid-October, after U.S. air attacks had begun against Taliban and al Qaeda targets in Afghanistan, local newspapers revealed that Singapore intelligence officials had uncovered an attempt to recruit local Muslims who had been instructed to form a terrorist cell and be prepared for war when called upon. The Singaporeans had refused,[6] and there was a sense of relief that the island was not involved in this kind of pointless violence.

The next day, however, Lee Kuan Yew addressed the issue of rising Islamist militancy: "They are broadening the appeal to all Muslims worldwide to fight on their behalf. . . . This is one huge propaganda assault to intimidate all the moderates in the Muslim world into silence so that they become the voice of the Muslim world. Are we exempt from this? If you believe that, you're sadly mistaken."[7]

Lee would ultimately be proved correct. Singapore was not exempt. Still, its proactive approach to resolving ethnic diversity, its prosperity, and internal vigilance would make Singapore more resistant than other Southeast Asian countries to the entreaties of those who sought to divide its peoples. It had been exemplary from its birth as a nation in refusing to cater exclusively to the interests of its ethnic Chinese majority. In 1965, Singapore was cast out from Malaysia as an independent country amid deadly ethnic violence between Chinese and Malays. Lee Kuan Yew would later write that he was "determined to make it clear to all, in particular the Chinese, now the majority, that the government would enforce the law impartially regardless of race or religion."[8] The country, given little chance to survive, would be best served by convincing the three main ethnic groups, each with its own religions, traditions, and prejudices, that their best chance was to live and develop together, to strive to improve their educational levels and become one people with a national identity they could at first only imagine. It would take time for them to begin feeling like Singaporeans.

The thoughts and emotions of the larger Islamic community in the aftermath of September 11 were still unknown territory, for the most part. Shamim had made a pilgrimage to Mecca with a group of Muslims led by a cleric named Ustaz Abdul Aziz Mohamad. She helped arrange a meeting at his mosque in the eastern reaches of the city-state. My yellow-top taxi swooped through grassy fields clumped with apartment blocks, past a stadium—Home of the Tampines Rovers soccer team—behind which rose a slender, modern tower embossed with a crescent star, a mosque. I disembarked at a walkway near double doors opening into a broad prayer room, where a solitary bearded man read intently from a Koran, displaying no interest in me or in anything except the words before him. To the left, a glass door opened into an office where a receptionist covered with a blue pastel *tudung* gestured at a wooden chair with a thin cushion, a functional piece of office furniture in keeping with the character of the mosque, which lacked the traditional dome. Aziz would be a few minutes, she said in the vaguely harried manner of all secretaries. A thick book, *Among the Believers*, by V.S. Naipaul, created a lump in my brown leather bag. It would have been enjoyable to read a few pages while waiting, but as I was sitting precisely where the title indicated and feared that it might create some offense, the book remained where it was. There had been a story in a newspaper that week about an Islamic group protesting Naipaul's Nobel Prize for literature because he was critical of their religion. A Nobel spokesman had replied that the writer was quite evenhanded in that he considered all religions to be the scourge of mankind. Naipaul's trenchant analysis of an extremism that wanted to bring down the modern state and substitute for it some un-specified Islamist plan was interesting. This brand of Islam, he had written, "appeared to raise political issues. But it had the flaw of its origins—the flaw that ran right through Islamic history to the political issues it raised: it offered no political or practical solution. It offered only the faith. It offered only the

Prophet, who would settle everything—but who had ceased to exist. This political Islam was rage, anarchy."[9] The corner of a page was turned down midway through a chapter about Islam in Malaysia that might offer some illumination of the religion in Singapore. My fingers felt for the ridged contours of the book beneath the thick leather, just as Aziz appeared, a slight man with crooked rimless glasses and a dark fringe of beard, wearing a white robe and skullcap that could not contain wisps of unruly hair. I shook his thin hand and he showed me to a cubicle with a lighted computer screen at his left, gesturing to another chair much like the first. Aziz had attended public school in Singapore, then studied Arabic and the Koran for six years in Saudi Arabia. He was both an *imam*, who led prayers in the mosque, and an *ustaz*, or a theological teacher. He was a serious man, there were demands on his energies and we should not dally.

No time for small talk. Fair enough. There had been disturbances, murmurs of jihad in neighboring Indonesia and Malaysia in retaliation for U.S. bombing recently begun in Afghanistan, and yet in Singapore the Muslim community remained quiescent. Why was it different?

Aziz looked wide-eyed through his thick glasses and said in a soft voice that Muslims in Singapore had jobs and decent incomes, and since the 1970s, they had lived not in their native *kampung* communities, but in racially integrated flats built by the government that they purchased and often improved to add value to their fortunes. They were nearly all property owners with their personal stakes in the country. Also, there had been the Religious Harmony Act, which made it illegal for any race, ethnic or religious group to say derogatory things about others or to incite strife between the groups.

"The Koran tells us that mankind is made into nations and tribes that we may know one another," Aziz said, his eyes shining. "So that we may know one another . . ." He lingered over the phrase. "The most honorable among you is one who has God consciousness, not because you are Arab, or American, or you are Malay, you are Chinese, but because you have God consciousness." His unfocused eyes gleamed with delight.

What did he think of creating an Islamist state?

The slightest hesitation was followed by affirmation. "Yes, it is a good thing that a state should be based upon the wisdom that is in the Koran," Aziz said.

What if most people, for example, ethnic Chinese and Indians, did not want to live in an Islamist state?

"Then we must try to educate them," Aziz said, with perfect logic, "to show them the beauty of Islam."

And what if they still did not want to live in an Islamist state? Was he willing to accept that?

Again the hesitation. "Yes," Aziz said, sadly, as though I had said something that was faintly absurd. "We would accept that."

Like many of the fundamentalist Christians I had encountered earlier in life, Aziz was utterly convinced of his truth; he had found it and everyone else must have the opportunity to find their salvation in it as well. There was only a thin line between this view and fanaticism, but Aziz kept himself on the good side of it. He may have been blasted with God consciousness, but his priorities were appropriately ordered. He claimed that all people should submit their wills to Allah, but he did not demand that they do so. Aziz did not descend into religious fascism, nor did he seem to devalue those who lived outside the borders of his flock of believers.

People like Aziz were the reason that terms such as "Islamic fundamentalists," when used to refer to terrorists, could be misleading. Several Muslims have pointed out that murderous acts perpetrated by al Qaeda are really not Islamic, because they are forbidden in the Koran. The more political term "militant Islamists," meaning those who seek through violence to impose their version of an Islamic state on others, seems more accurate, and also demarcates clearly a threshold that separates good from evil, which can be a useful concept to bear in mind in a confusing world. Referring to such people simply as "terrorists" may be adequate for most usages. The final term that we should consider is "jihad," which can mean simply to strive within oneself to follow the religion of Islam. Others, including terrorists, have taken as their personal "jihad" the waging of an armed conflict, a holy war that is meant to expel outsiders and establish a pure Islamist state. It is in this latter sense that we shall use the word here, because it is the reality we must confront.

As war raged in Afghanistan, Shamim said she was experiencing some confusion about her identity, but her thinking had become clear about the suicide hijackers and militant Islamists: "Those guys are nuts," she declared, strengthened in loyalty to her family, friends, and country that contained and nurtured her life and her aspirations.

The same war prompted a dialogue with a young British expatriate academic, a tall, gangly fellow with a thin, hawkish face and a shock of floppy hair who insisted the United States would accomplish nothing and probably lose the conflict, much as it had in Vietnam, and that it ought to negotiate with the terrorists, as Britain had done in Northern Ireland,

and because perhaps the terrorists had some point of justice on their side simply because the United States was large and imperially powerful and therefore deserved to receive a comeuppance. This was my first experience of overt anti-Americanism, but there would be more of this hopeful *schadenfreude* among the European crowd. Those who understood terrorism and had worked out effective ways to deal with it, he said, knew that it could be handled only through protracted negotiations. An American attempt to fight the Taliban in Afghanistan was not only morally wrong, but was doomed to fail.

Was he a pacifist then? I asked.

Nope, he was just offering me the benefit of his accumulated knowledge. Americans possessed no real strategic sense, but were hopeless cowboys in the international arena. By going to war in Afghanistan, it was quite obvious that a thousand new Osamas would be created to bedevil the world in the future. The answer was clear: negotiations.

The problem was, unlike the Irish Republican Army, which at least showed a small measure of common humanity in that it had often phoned ahead before its bombs exploded, al Qaeda sought no communication with its enemy. Bin Laden's teacher and colleague, Dr. Abdullah Azzam, had articulated a doctrine of "jihad and the rifle alone; no negotiations, no conferences and no dialogues."[10] It was possible that the Briton's view was based on experience, although given his relative youth that was unlikely. He seemed awash in the sort of cultural relativity that had marked tolerant, liberal thought worldwide during the decades of Soviet-inspired revolutions that followed after the Vietnam War from Cambodia to Nicaragua. Because one man's terrorist was just another man's freedom fighter, there could be no actual standards of good and evil. It was an easy-to-understand, if questionable, mode of thought that had been invalidated by September 11 and was fading into a blur of history. It also exemplified what bin Laden had assumed he would find among Westerners, a lack of mettle; spoiled, unmotivated people with no stomach for a fight even when they were attacked. The Americans, al Qaeda operatives often said, could be easily defeated through guerrilla tactics and would pull out after incurring a few casualties. The terrorists were emboldened to attack because they thought they had perceived weakness, and if they found that to be true, they would be encouraged to increase the intensity of their assault. These were not the best of times for theories, nor were they suitable for the trendy postures of political irony and cynicism that had become fashionable in the untroubled decade leading up to September 11. These had become serious times when an intensification of priorities demanded a more realistic approach to life.

Al Qaeda did not encounter the American weakness they had expected in Afghanistan, where the U.S. military combined with the anti-Taliban Northern Alliance to fight a short, effective war and scatter most of the surviving terrorists into the mountains along Pakistan's ungoverned frontier territory, where in a disrupted condition they continued operations, perhaps still believing that if they lost their lives, they would gain immediate access to paradise as their reward for slaying infidels. This was not a banal evil, as we find in Hannah Arendt's description of the efficient bureaucracy employed for mass murder by the Nazis; it was a madness that afflicted human beings who had willingly mistaken bad for good, who had listened like Macbeth to the ambiguities of the witches and followed a course of evil. The terrorists had been seized by a pathological desire to "purify" the world as well as to preserve themselves in some imaginary paradise where they could eternally deflower scores of dark-eyed virgins.

This was a deadly irrational frustration stemming from a broad disappointment that the flower of Islam's golden age had wilted into the stagnant cultures and nations we find in the Middle East today, that a people had descended from historical predominance into contemporary insignificance. If Muslims were the true people of the one God, they asked, then why had they fallen as the West had ascended? Finding an answer to this question, the scholar Bernard Lewis wrote, may lie in ceasing to blame the West for the decline and instead focusing on how to put things right within Islam.

Two paths ostensibly reaching toward this end have emerged, a first that seeks to move forward, while the second is backward-looking. Secular democracy like that we see in Turkey or a capitalist developmental strategy such as Malaysia has employed would seem to be promising ways for predominantly Islamic nations to move ahead. The second path is regressive, leading back toward a legendary past, as we have seen in both the Iranian revolution and in the rigid, Islamist extremism that has emerged and been packaged for export in Saudi Arabia, which has become well known as Wahhabism.

Unfortunately, this path of regression is being followed by a hardcore minority. The origin of al Qaeda's roots can be found in what is now Saudi Arabia, with the birth in 1703 of radical cleric Muhammad ibn Abd al-Wahhab. The writer Stephen Schwartz said that "the real source of our problem is in the perversion of Islamic teachings by the fascistic Wahhabi cult that resides at the heart of the Saudi establishment, our putative friends in the region."[11]

The Wahhabist doctrine was conceived in the harsh Arabian desert, far from modernism, the Industrial Revolution, and developments that were transforming the outside world. In their isolation, Wahhabis grew fearful of what they perceived as a threatening force emanating from the land of the "crusaders," and to the world's great misfortune they received an ideological transfusion from the reactionary jihadist ideas of Sayyid Qutb, who argued that an Islamist state under Shariah law was necessary to achieve the true Islam of past glories. Armed jihad, he insisted, was the only way to realize such a state. An organization of Muslims committed to the creation of a totally pure nation, therefore, must bring it into existence, and all those who did not share their vision, including most other Muslims, could legitimately be killed. This combination of rigid Wahhabism arising in isolation and the incendiary writings of Qutb and other radical Islamists converged with another facilitating factor, which was big money. After the oil shocks of the mid-1970s, Saudi Arabia found that the price increases of crude oil left it awash in petrodollars, and scores of billions were diverted to spread the ideology of militant jihad around the world, to Pakistan, Afghanistan, the Philippines, Indonesia, Malaysia, and to Singapore. The spearhead is al Qaeda, and in Southeast Asia its affiliate Jemaah Islamiyah carries out its acts of terror.

"The Saudis, both government-sponsored organizations and wealthy individuals, have exported a puritanical and at times militant version of Wahhabi Islam to other countries and communities in the Muslim world," the scholar John L. Esposito wrote, adding that "wealthy businessmen in Saudi

Arabia, both members of the establishment and outsiders such as Osama bin Laden, have provided financial support to extremist groups who follow a militant fundamentalist brand of Islam with its jihad culture."[12]

Lewis wrote that "the suicide bomber may become a metaphor for the whole region, and there will be no escape from a downward spiral of hate and spite, rage and self-pity, poverty and oppression."[13] This is not a pleasant view of the future, and as he went on to note, the ultimate choice belongs to Muslims themselves. Some people, Middle Eastern intellectuals among them, speak hopefully of a Reformation of Islam that might be similar to the movement in the sixteenth century that curbed many excesses of the Roman Catholic Church and led to the establishment of Protestant Christianity.

Reaching some small understanding of Islamist terrorism's sources in Saudi Arabia and its migration to South Asia began to help unravel the mystery of who these people were. It was illuminating to discover that there was a puritanical religious and educational structure in Saudi Arabia in which separatism from other peoples and religions and the absolute superiority of their sect and its eventual conquest of the world were guiding precepts. How coldly puritanical were they? In March 2002, Saudi religious police forced fleeing students at a Mecca girls' school back inside a burning building because they were not properly attired in headscarves and robes. That the girls died in the fire was of secondary importance to the Wahhabis. Because the United States is dependent on Saudi oil and because there is a well-paid lobby that looks after Saudi interests in Washington, this religious establishment with its dangerous ideology and actions was never closely examined until brought to the attention of the world by the September 11 attacks, in which most of the suicide hijackers were Saudis.

The Wahhabis had been able to bring under their influence a group of ethnic Pashtun studying at Saudi-funded *madrassas,* or Islamic schools, in Pakistan, who became known as the Taliban. Many Southeast Asian Muslims who went to Afghanistan to help out in the anti-Soviet struggle also came under Wahhabi influence and returned home ablaze with Islamist extremism that prepared them to commit acts of terror.

As Schwartz wrote, "Wahhabism exalts and promotes death in every element of its existence: the suicide of its adherents, mass murder as a weapon against civilization, and above all the suffocation of the mercy embodied in Islam. The war against terrorist Wahhabism is therefore a war to the death, as the Second World War was a war to the death against fascism."[14]

There will be no quarter asked or given by terrorists filled with such motivations. Their totalitarian beliefs allow only for victory or martyrdom, and while their chances of victory are small, the number of innocent people they slay in their jihad will be decided by the strength of the West's resolve to defend itself, a quality about which there may still be some doubt.

TERROR in SINGAPORE

EARLY 2002—JUST AFTER NEW YEAR'S, THE SINGAPORE GOVERN-
MENT ANNOUNCED THAT IT HAD JAILED THIRTEEN TERRORISTS, MANY
OF WHOM HAD TRAINED IN AL QAEDA CAMPS IN AFGHANISTAN. It
intended to detain them for two-year terms under the Internal Security Act, charging they were members of a regional
Islamist organization called Jemaah Islamiyah (JI). The Ministry of Home Affairs said JI had carried out surveillance and
was planning to bomb Western embassies, including that of
the United States, as well as a mass transit station where they
would have killed many ordinary Singaporeans, including
Muslims, presumably. It also said they were linked to militants in Malaysia and Indonesia, and that some of the group
had escaped capture.

Singapore's security service named an Indonesian cleric,

schoolmaster, and supporter of Osama bin Laden named Abu Bakar Bashir as the spiritual leader of Jemaah Islamiyah. Bashir admitted that he had taught some of the detainees, but denied any personal involvement in terrorism. He said that the United States was really the terrorist nation. After the September 11 attacks, he had "rejoiced, because it seemed Allah punished the United States for its arrogant behavior."[1] Indonesia, home to several powerful Islamic political organizations, vacillated, but ultimately declined to arrest Bashir, citing a lack of evidence.

The guru of the Singapore cell was an innocuous apartment manager named Ibrahim Maidin. Pictures of all the jihadis were published on the front pages of local newspapers. One long-haired, bearded young man named Mohamad Nazir looked more like a hippie than a terrorist. Whom could you trust these days?

Malaysian police also rounded up numerous militants, uncovering a group with links to Zacarias Moussaoui, the French national charged in the United States with conspiracy related to the September 11 attacks.

A man called Hambali was identified as the operational commander of Jemaah Islamiyah, but he wiggled through the nets of both nations' security forces. Hambali, to the misfortune of many, would be heard from again.

Muslim leaders in Singapore stood behind the government crackdown. "We should support efforts to extinguish extremism within our midst and protect the interests of the vast majority of Muslims and also of our fellow Singaporeans," Yaacob Ibrahim, a Muslim cabinet minister, told a Hari Raya holiday tea party at a local hotel after the end of the month-long Ramadan fast.[2]

The next week, the government released more information. The jihadi suspects had kept low profiles, much like the September 11 group in the United States. Eight of them had been to Afghanistan for training in weapons and assassination techniques. A videotape of potential Singapore targets, presumably made by the detainees and including transport centers where U.S. military personnel might be killed, had been found by American troops in Afghanistan and was shown on Singapore television. Jemaah Islamiyah had obtained several tons of nitrate fertilizer with which to make truck bombs of explosive power that could have dwarfed the Oklahoma City blast.[3] The terrorists had planned to accumulate more than twenty tons of the chemical, which could have laid waste to a good portion of Singapore had they succeeded.

One man who knew a great deal about this group was Rohan Gunaratna, author of the book *Inside Al Qaeda*, and a former research fellow at the Centre for the Study of Terrorism and Political Violence at University of St. Andrews, Scotland, who was looking into al Qaeda's activities in Southeast Asia. Gunaratna was working with Singapore's Institute of Defence and Strategic Studies, where he is head of Terrorism Research, as well as consulting with the United Nations. He is a stocky, gruff Sri Lankan who chooses his words carefully. He said he had been drawn to the terrorism field by the troubles in his home country. We spoke early one steamy morning at his three-story row house in Singapore. I wondered if the roundup of Jemaah Islamiyah terrorists had been a case of getting lucky, or was it a result of good security?

Gunaratna collected his thoughts for a moment, then spoke in a rapid monotone: "The guardians of security in Singapore are the Internal Security Department (ISD). This agency has a reputation both in this region and outside it for its professionalism. It is the enduring sense of security that is embedded in the minds of the ISD staff that really enabled it to be the first agency in Southeast Asia to detect the presence of the al Qaeda terrorist network." Gunaratna and others had been aware for some time that al Qaeda was active in Southeast Asia, but no one realized the extensive nature and structure of the organization in the region until the ISD had unearthed it.

Singapore appeared to be a prosperous country. Unlike the situation in Pakistan or in certain Middle Eastern states, there were no large numbers of unemployed, frustrated young men floating around, available to be recruited into terrorist groups. Why, then, did he suppose terrorism existed in a country where people's aspirations were not thwarted, where it was possible for them to realize their dreams if they work hard?

Gunaratna looked perplexed, as if the answer was obvious. "The root cause of terrorism is not poverty or lack of literacy," he said. "The real motivation is not lack of employment. It is ideology, that is, the belief system of a religious group. Right now, Islamism has great appeal, so it is natural for an extremist interpretation to be supported by so many youths who believe that Muslims are being discriminated against and that Islam cannot be practiced in secular countries, so they are trying to create Islamist states. The Singapore Muslims are no exception to this trend." This was all in his book, Gunaratna said.

I could see that, but it still seemed that in nations such as Indonesia and the Philippines, corruption, poverty, and sheer boredom were probably factors that lead discontented young men to accept the ideology preached by the extremist clerics and brought about their participation in terrorism.

Singapore, however, was prosperous. It was also a multiethnic society. What role did that play?

"To a large extent, Southeast Asian Muslims are moderate and tolerant because they have lived under the shadow of large Buddhist, Christian, Hindu, and other communities. The Singaporean Muslims are very moderate, but in every society there is a radical fringe. Jemaah Islamiyah, which is al Qaeda's Southeast Asian network, targeted those Muslims and recruited, indoctrinated, and trained them."

Was this a situation similar to a religious cult?

"These groups are secretive and have some similarities to cults. They belong to an elite, small organization that operates in secrecy. Terrorist organizations also are politically driven, even though they have the garb of religion."

What did the internal command structure of Jemaah Islamiyah look like?

"It is a mirror image of the al Qaeda structure. Above Ibrahim Maidin, the spiritual leader of the Singapore group, were people like Hambali, Bashir, and Osama bin Laden."

In the environment of Afghanistan, the command structure could be open and known to everyone, like any military organization, but wasn't it more secretive in Singapore? Perhaps a cellular structure in which members were not necessarily aware of each other or of their leaders?

"These people knew they were part of al Qaeda's organization. They went to Afghanistan and trained in al Qaeda camps, and many of them also trained in al Qaeda–built camps in Mindanao in the Philippines."

Would local members have known from whom Ibrahim Maidin was receiving his orders?

"Certainly."

This seemed uncertain to me, actually, but Gunaratna seemed to have little doubt about the point, so I moved on to my next question. How did he see the Jemaah Islamiyah structure in terms of the Southeast Asian region?

"It is a regional organization, not a Singaporean organization. It was created in 1972 in Indonesia. By 1978, the leadership relocated to Malaysia, established links with al Qaeda in 1987 when Hambali went to Afghanistan and trained and fought until 1991. Then he returned to Malaysia and helped build JI into a regional network that extended even as far as Australia. Singapore is but one part of that network."

What was Bashir's function in this group?

"Bashir is the spiritual, political, and ideological leader. He also has some operational role. The key operational commander is Hambali. He serves in the consultational councils of both JI and al Qaeda, so he holds dual membership."

What did Jemaah Islamiyah want? What were they trying to attain?

"They want to create an Islamist state in Southeast Asia. The radicalized Muslims believe they cannot live as true Muslims in a non-Islamist state, and that is why they want to return to the generation of the Prophet, when the companions of the Prophet lived, and that was the Caliphate. They want to go back to that. They want to create these Islamist states, lift the borders, unify and create the Caliphates. They want no separation of politics and religion. They want to impose Shariah law."

I wondered what intentions Jemaah Islamiyah might have for the other peoples who presently occupied these regions, if they were somehow able to take control of them. The thought frightened me.

After the detention of Jemaah Islamiyah members, the head of a local Islamic organization that sponsored a Web site called fateha.com criticized Singapore's leaders through foreign media channels. Zulfikar Mohamad Shariff made his opinions known when he was interviewed by various international media, including the BBC, and by mid-January, Muslim member of parliament Yatiman Yusof responded with three points: First, Zulfikar claimed to be a leader of the Muslim community while saying that elected parliamentarians were not; second, Zulfikar claimed that Jemaah Islamiyah's actions were prompted by the Singapore government aligning itself with the United States and Israel; and, third, Zulfikar questioned whether members of Jemaah Islamiyah were actually terrorists. The parliamentarian said it was clear from Zulfikar's Internet postings that he was "fighting for the creation of a purist Muslim society without due regard to the multi-racial and multi-religious Singapore,"[4] adding that he was trying to bring Muslims into conflict with other Singaporeans and with other Muslims as well, and that the community should move to isolate him.

Then in February, a related issue surfaced that involved the *tudung* headscarf worn by some Muslim women. Parents of four primary-school girls had insisted their children wear the headscarf to school, which is not allowed in Singapore. In the government's view, school is a common space, while the headscarf encourages religious segregation. Prime Minister Goh Chok Tong said that two of the girls would be suspended if they showed up in headscarves the next day, that a third girl had already withdrawn from school, while the parents of the fourth were being counseled. Three of the cases were politically motivated, Goh told a Mendaki gathering, and the person behind the agitation was the head of a local Web site, a fellow named Zulfikar.[5]

A few days later, the mufti of Singapore said that education was a higher priority than wearing the headscarf, but his advice was rejected by the fathers of two of the girls.[6] Days later, as Chinese New Year approached, Goh asked that ethnic Chinese Singaporeans invite Muslim friends to celebrate with them, and urged Muslims to reject extremists and to continue participating in the city-state's racial and religious harmony, building on what they had already accomplished "to achieve our dream of a successful multiracial, multireligious Singapore family."[7]

These events made it clear that Zulfikar figured in the battle for the hearts and minds of the island's Muslims, and that some understanding of him would be of value. I decided to seek him out the following week, but before that, there was another man who had also become of interest: Syed Farid Alatas, a sociology professor at the National University of Singapore who had spoken at a recent Inter-Civilization Dialogue, an event conceived as a response to Huntington's clash of civilizations thesis. This year, there had been plenty to talk about. Farid was articulate in his explanation of Islam and took pains to point out that more people had died in secular wars in the past century than in religious conflicts, which was true enough, but it seemed to me that since September 11, we had entered into a new century, maybe a new age. He invited me to his office for a chat over the weekend.

National University was up a tree-covered hill from our

house on Pasir Panjang Road, which ran along what had once been a long strand of sandy beach. It was now a row of automated container port cranes from which we were separated by a green strip of park. I set out walking in the midday heat and arrived about fifteen minutes later. Farid was a tall man with black hair and a neatly trimmed beard streaked with gray. He said his family name was of Arab origin. Farid's office was furnished in typical utilitarian academic style with a wall of books and a desk in the back. There was also a handsome Oriental carpet and two chairs for visitors. Perspiring from the walk, I sat down, wiped my brow and gathered my breath. Farid sat back, his fingers touching, eyeing me from behind his desk. I asked if it had been difficult for Singapore, with its three ethnic groups and the problems associated with this, to forge a national identity and a successful economy.

"I think in any society that is multicultural, multiethnic, and multireligious," Farid said, pausing thoughtfully, "you will have problems. Even in democracies you have serious problems such as racial violence, riots, and discrimination on a daily basis. People are no different here. Singapore has tried to overcome this through less-than-liberal policies, which are not necessarily a negative thing. They are less than liberal in the sense that the ideal of free speech, for example, is qualified by the need to maintain racial and religious harmony, so certain topics are off limits." If people had complaints regarding race or religion, Farid said, they were expected to bring them up with officials privately, rather than by having open discussions with the foreign media.

This, I took as a broad implication that included the recent actions of Zulfikar, but we would get to that presently.

Did Singaporeans lose through this approach, I asked, or did they gain?

Farid thought Singaporeans gained. "There would only be a loss if these restrictions were extended to other areas, and I think they are sometimes, by people misunderstanding them, which becomes self-censorship, so there is a loss in that sense. I don't think the loss is in terms of lack of harmony. Whatever harmony there is has a lot to do with the laws in place."

It was a trade-off then, so it seemed that the question might be rephrased: Did the good that the island's people derived from these laws outweigh the resulting lack of freedoms?

"Yes, and these are freedoms relating to expression. The lack of them does not mean it's impossible to engage in discourse with the government, but the channels of discourse are not the same as those you have in liberal democracies."

There were channels available?

"I think there are. Malay members of parliament say that if there is discrimination, they want to hear about it. Then if the problem continues, you have a case, and if you go to the foreign media, we'll be exposed. They say that. I think that's fair. So, one means of maintaining harmony is through law, and the other is through a flourishing economy, and these help to keep whatever tensions there might be submerged."

Some economists said that much of what we generally thought of as freedom might actually be attributed to the privileges granted by economic development, that access to a decent life, raising your family with adequate medical care, and living in modern housing were important components of freedom.

"Yes, so you have serious racial tensions and violence in the United States because of economic inequality."

That could not be denied. Farid knew something about the United States, having received his doctorate at Johns Hopkins more than ten years earlier. We were diminishing it, though, the racial separation and economic inequality, one painful step at a time. And still, it remained as part of American life.

"Inequality in Singapore doesn't take the form of ghettos. We have some inequality, but people are not hungry."

Still, Malay-Muslims didn't make as much money as the ethnic Chinese or Indian segments of the population. Why was that?

"I think it goes back to colonial times, to the fact that Malays were mostly agricultural people, and when the British came the Malays were not brought into the urban sector; in fact, there were laws that served to keep them on the land, and there were laws that didn't allow the Chinese to buy land, so that forced them into an urban environment. That's probably part of it."

That also helped explain why urban Singapore came to have a large ethnic Chinese majority. How would he rate the performance of Lee Kuan Yew over the past four decades?

Singaporeans owed everything they had to Lee, in Farid's view. "When his People's Action Party came to power, I think Lee and his team decided to run this country differently than other countries in the region. The commitment to say that we were not going to be corrupt, we were going to be efficient, we were going to apply these rules and regulations seriously and be unflinching about it. I think that's what did it. You have this kind of rhetoric everywhere, but he actually did it. Perhaps the problem is that along with the commitment came a sort of cold, technocratic approach to culture, to ideas, and maybe that was a negative part."

Farid seemed to be a complex man, with undercurrents running beneath a surface of quiet reserve. A colleague had told me his father was a noted professor as well. Farid's perceptions were helpful in shining light on Singaporean culture and Islam within it. What of the terrorist attacks of September 11, I asked, and the effect they might have had on racial harmony in Singapore?

The attacks had not damaged racial harmony, but they made people realize that the word "harmony" was vacuous. "It means that people are not fighting with each other," Farid said, his words beginning to stream more smoothly along as he rose to the subject. "The other term that people use is 'tolerance.' But I think it brought home the point that tolerance is not enough. Tolerance implies a grudging acceptance of each other, and harmony based on tolerance is precarious, because anything could upset the balance. There needs to be more than tolerance. There needs to be mutual understanding, respect, interest in each other's religions and cultures. And there has been more recent awareness of that." There had been interfaith dialogues, more visits to places of worship, such as mosques and temples, and more publicity. Even so, this seemed to trouble him, as thought it were still not enough. There were deeper reasons for these troubles.

I'd read in a newspaper article that Cabinet Minister Yaacob Ibrahim said it was a challenge to be a good Muslim as well as a good citizen. What did that mean?

"I suppose there are things that you might be called upon to do as a citizen that might go against your religion. For an extreme example, going to war against Malaysia, where you would have to kill fellow Muslims."

In that case, is your primary identity as a Muslim or as a

Singaporean stronger? Who are you? What would happen?

"Well, that's part of the question. It's not really discussed in the open. Generally, the Malays say that it's not a simple thing. I've heard Malays say that if Singapore were invaded by the Malaysian army, Singapore's as much their home as it is for the Chinese, and they'd defend it. I don't think they're taking the view that if Malaysian Muslims attack them, they're going to put down their weapons simply because they are also Muslims."

Yes, but there was a certain problem in Singapore's armed forces, wasn't there? Malays were seldom trusted enough to be allowed to rise to high positions?

"In the past, many Malays were not even called to serve, although this has been changing. Some Malays resent this, because they feel that they were here even before the Chinese."

I wondered just how deep this resentment ran. What did Farid make of the Jemaah Islamiyah arrests and the destructive plans that some rather economically comfortable Singaporeans seemed to have been making?

You simply could not relate economic and political conditions of Muslims in Singapore to Jemaah Islamiyah, Farid said. In a situation where there was pronounced inequality, it would be easy to see why such things might occur, for example, in the context of the poverty and corruption of Indonesia, or with Abu Saayaf in the Philippines. In the case of Singapore, the militant group did not reflect the conditions of the larger Muslim community, so the reasons had to be sought elsewhere. Exactly where that might be, Farid could only speculate. There was misplaced zeal and a need by people to be integrated into a group, much as we saw with the Jonestown cult in 1978, when 914 members of the Peoples

Temple died in murder-suicides in Guyana. These groups integrated their members so deeply that they were willing to die for each other. There was some of that going on with Jemaah Islamiyah, and he thought that the suicide bombers on September 11 were similar. They were brought into the group, and a few days before they performed their final acts, they were not left alone; people stayed with them to ensure they did not deviate from their missions.

Those missions were meant to demonstrate a sort of spiritual heroism and martyrdom in order to bring about an earthshaking political change. What did Farid think of the concept of an Islamist state?

"It's a concept," he said, shrugging. "But there's no blueprint for it. The people who are talking about founding such states are speaking mostly about imposing Shariah law, but when they say they want to apply it, they are speaking of a few things such as women wearing veils, banning of alcohol, and things like that. But many things that did not exist in the time of the Prophet, such as modern banking systems, are not dealt with. Can you allow a dual banking system? Can you allow conventional banks? These things have never been resolved."

What, I wondered, were Farid's thoughts about the Web site fateha.com?

"I have problems with what they've been doing," Farid said, scowling faintly. Fateha.com had done a disservice to Singapore and to Muslims. It had linked the arrest of the detainees to dissatisfaction within the Muslim community, which gave the impression that Muslims in Singapore were generally unhappy and that the thirteen men planning to do evil things were a product of that community, which was not true. "If the Singapore government had policies that resulted in the extreme poverty of the Malays, crime, and ghettos, then there would be hatred for the government, but that's not happening. It is wrong to make such a connection."

Did Farid think that Zulfikar represented Muslims in Singapore? Did he have a real constituency?

He did not, although there might be some who felt he did regarding the *tudung* issue, which was not so simple. "On the surface, it looks like a straightforward matter of religious freedom. Why not allow anyone to do this, right? From my point of view, and that of some other Muslims, it's good that the government doesn't allow it, because a lot of parents would force their six-year-old kids to wear them. The kids have no defense. I don't want people to be forcing their kids to cover their hair, especially small children. Maybe later, at sixteen or seventeen, they can make their own decisions."

What of the Muslim political leaders in Singapore? Were they doing a good job, or were they failing the community?

Yaacob Ibrahim, the minister for Muslim affairs, was Farid's friend. Some of the Malay members of parliament were also his friends and he met with them regularly. "It's difficult to generalize about them. I think many of them are working behind the scenes, and as a result they are seen as not doing anything, or as being too compliant to the PAP [People's Action Party]. Also, I think the Malay population probably doesn't use them enough, doesn't approach them enough to deal with their problems and grouses. Actually, Singapore's government is better than that of most Muslim countries."

I thought about that statement, and began thumbing through a mental catalogue of governments from the Middle

East to Africa to South and Southeast Asia, trying to think of one that exceeded it in providing for the common good of its people.

Leaving Farid's office, following the grassy contours of the hillside while keeping as much as possible within the shady envelope cast by trees in the harsh midday sun, I found myself thinking about the meanings of words such as "moderate," "fundamentalist," and "extremist." Was a moderate Muslim lax in his observances, or was Islam properly understood as religion of moderation? Did a fundamentalist Muslim read the Koran literally, without interpretation in the way that fundamentalist Christians professed to read the Bible? Was a Muslim who strictly followed the words of the Koran a person who went to extremes, or was he admonished by the text not to adopt extreme views? As a person who had arrived in Singapore a couple years earlier with little understanding of Islam, these were questions that would require research and much more comprehension. One thing that had become obvious, however, was that terrorists had moved beyond all of these categories. They operated covertly, trying to create an Islamist state by mayhem and murder. Still, they were convinced that their mission was sacred. They had been persuaded by their own clerics—who had promised them the paradise of the martyrs—to sacrifice even their lives for the group's political cause. In accepting the illusions conjured by radical clerics, the terrorists had crossed over the line that divides sanity from pathology.

These organizations had become death cults that fashioned believers into tools to commit evil in the name of God without pausing to consider even briefly how unlikely it was that a virtuous God would require such acts. This was where the militant clerics made their appearance, stepping into the space between God and humanity to minister to those who were unable to make spiritual connections for themselves. The clerics convinced malleable and needy believers to surrender their wills to God, and to prove that surrender through actions that confirmed the authority of the clerics. This seduction was carried out by interpreting sacred texts to justify political motivations and aims, and then through the gradual transfer of reverence for God to the words of the clerics themselves. Were these methods of control used by Bashir at his Mukmin boarding school for jihad on crowded Java island, and by Maidin with the Singapore terrorists? "With surrender, the authority of the leader is maximized, the follower feels relieved of uncertainty and choice and can experience the 'bliss' of someone who has 'returned home.'"[8] Critical thinking and judgment were set aside. In such a pliable state, the believers could ever more ardently feel and respond to clerical authority as they gradually lost contact with the last wispy strands of their previous realities. The cleric's causes became their own, and violent acts were celebrated as having been committed in the service of the Almighty.

Those who belonged to the secretive in-group and served its ends were seen as good. Outsiders were demonized, so that any act of violence or cruelty could be committed against them and construed as acceptable or even virtuous. When outsiders, infidels, were thoroughly devalued, they could be portrayed as enemies without morals, people who hardly deserved to live and therefore could be killed with no twinge of conscience. Their deaths could be laughed at. Murder could be viewed through lenses of twisted self-righteousness.

Consider a statement by the late Ayatollah Ruhollah Khomeini of Iran: "If one permits an infidel to continue in his role as a corrupter of the earth, his moral suffering will be all the worse. If one kills the infidel, and thus stops him from perpetrating his misdeeds, his death will be a blessing to him."[9] Through such convolutions of reason, Islamist clerics had been able to turn their followers' minds around until they could view slaughter and serial killing as sacred acts. The word "prejudice" seems insufficient to convey the hyperintensity of their group identification and their loathing for outsiders. In modern times, perhaps only the most insular hate merchants such as the Nazis or the imperial Japanese had managed to attain such stunning depravity.

A common acquaintance provided Zulfikar's handphone number. He was amenable to a meeting at Funan Center, a downtown mall devoted to computers and accessories. There was a glassed-in coffee shop where we could talk.

The next week, as good as his word, Zulfikar sat across the table. He had rich brown skin, jet-black hair cut short, and a stylish, sparse goat beard. Although he had attended university in Hawaii, Zulfikar said he was a classic Singaporean in that he is equal parts Malay, Chinese, Indian, and Pakistani. His grin was infectious, exposing two blinding white rows of teeth, with what my mother used to call a chicken tooth, an extra incisor pushed forward in the top row. He smiled often and laughed easily, making occasional personal jokes with a wink that said you were getting a little more than the public Zulfikar, the "professional agitator." We were being watched and maybe photographed at that moment, and his phone and apartment were bugged, he said with a grin. Across the way we could see the new red-roofed, neocolonial Parliament Building, where the legislature was opening. I asked what he thought of Jemaah Islamiyah.

"The perception of Singaporeans is that they could have been targeted in the bombings. I concern myself with how the government played the issue up. I think they showed a videotape that could strike fear into people. And I do not know if Bashir is leading them in jihad."

This struck me as possibly a little defensive. Hadn't the videotape been found in Afghanistan?

"The claim is that they found the tape in Afghanistan," Zulfikar said, his voice conveying a certain skepticism.

Did he think that terrorism was permissible?

"No, we do not agree with terrorism, whoever it is performed by, including Bush, Sharon, or Mullah Omar. But the question is, do we have sufficient proof to claim that al Qaeda was directly responsible for the September 11 attacks? You may think we do, but we think that there is not."

I could not help but feel a little edgy about this. We saw cities attacked and buildings destroyed, thousands of people killed and mutilated, a direct act of war. Was this just a legal case?

"Well, Bush did offer to try Osama bin Laden. We believe that Mullah Omar did want to have Osama tried in another country, but then the U.S. started bombing."

Even if Osama had been tried, al Qaeda would still have been free to continue operating, committing acts of terror.

"You are looking at it as if al Qaeda were responsible for September 11."

Weren't they?

"What I'm saying is this: You look at trying Osama, but he is still innocent until proven guilty. A lot of people are still skeptical of the messages that were sent. Even in an act of war, you must get the proof out first. We do not see that there was enough credible evidence to justify the war. In most of the Gulf states, the belief is that Osama is not the one."

Even now?

"Yes."

This astonished me. That gave me reason, I said, to worry about the soundness of those people's thought processes. There was an awkward moment. It occurred to me that we would never agree on these things. Zulfikar was probably experiencing a similar realization. It didn't mean that I had to dislike him, however. I wondered how he would react to me, someone who was obviously in a camp other than his on the issue.

"We are worried about your thought processes," he said.

Fair enough. While I could respect his right to hold such opinions, I could not share them. The United States had decided there was ample evidence to defend itself by going to war against those who had attacked it. I asked Zulfikar if he favored an Islamic state.

"I have no problem with an Islamic state. Islam is complete. It covers every aspect of your life. It even tells you about governance and laws."

Which Islamic state would he use as a model?

"There is no Islamic state in the world. There is some disagreement as to whether democracy is compatible with Islam. I am not given to determine what is correct."

Could Singapore become an Islamic state?

"Being a minority, I don't see that to be possible. Aceh province in Indonesia is trying to become an Islamic state. They are implementing Shariah law for Muslims."

Some Malaysian states, ruled by Parti Islam SeMalaysia (PAS), were also trying to do this.

"For the PAS to do this, it would have to be in power at the federal level, which would mean that the population had accepted their proposal, that Malaysians declared, as a democracy, it is the system they want."

Long in control of a power base of Kelantan state led by the venerable Nik Aziz, PAS also won control of Terengganu state in 1999. It banned karaoke outlets, bars, unisex hair salons, and gaming. Later, the state assembly passed a code of Islamic law (*hudud*) that allows punishments such as "whipping, stoning and amputations for offenses including theft, adultery, and the consumption of alcohol."[10] The two state governments were at odds with the federal government of Prime Minister Mahathir Mohamad in this.

What did Zulfikar think of Mahathir's approach to governing Malaysia?

"Mahathir has outlived his time. So has Lee Kuan Yew. I used to support them, but I began to read books and understand the manipulations. The biggest influence was probably Reformasi (a movement for democratic change led by former deputy prime minister Anwar Ibrahim): I was working in Malaysia when Anwar was ousted, and I found myself questioning his dismissal. Even though I was a keen Mahathir and Lee Kuan Yew supporter then, I found my support to be at odds with my analysis."

Many people were still uncertain about the Anwar case, it seemed. Wasn't Singapore's government, however, generally fair?

"We have something called Racial Harmony Day, and for that you are allowed to put on the *tudung*. That is supposed to be the ideal, so if that is true, why can't you wear it every day? Then there are the *madrassas*, the Islamic schools. One of the things the government doesn't like is that students can't mix with the other races. But what about the Special Assistance Plan Chinese schools that teach culture and heritage? Why do they allow one and not the other? Muslims are only 15 percent of the population, so no matter where we go we will interact with the other races. Chinese culture is important and I don't mind that, but why the double standard?"

It could be seen that way.

"Also, Mandarin is promoted more than the Malay language."

But didn't that make sense? Weren't the ethnic Chinese a large majority in Singapore?

"Our language should be treated on the same level. Malaysia is one of the biggest trading partners, we are surrounded by Malay-speaking nations, and yet, you do not want people to speak Malay? On top of that, Malay is the national language of Singapore. There are four official languages: English, Mandarin, Malay, and Tamil, but Malay is the national language. The overpromotion of Mandarin has resulted in chauvinistic attitudes. We still read that companies advertising employment in newspaper classified ads often ask for Mandarin-speakers only."

That was an undeniable fact, and it was a practice that did not necessarily contribute to the social unity of the city-state. Perhaps, however, Singapore was looking to develop links with China for its future economic well-being.

"Well, you know, a Hong Kong businessman will go to China and come back with a suitcase full of cash, but a Singaporean will go to China and come back with a brief-case full of feasibility studies."

CHAPTER 3

We laughed. Singaporeans trying to enter the Chinese market had sometimes found their open and transparent business practices gave them little competitive advantage on the mainland, where a well-placed bribe might bring more immediate results. Perhaps Singaporeans weren't corrupt enough, but in any case, didn't he think that in four decades, Lee Kuan Yew had performed something almost miraculous in developing the country?

Economically, Zulfikar said, there was not much that you could fault. "What the government has going for it is the economy. If the economy stumbles and there are not enough foreign reserves to tide it over, I think you will see a lot more problems. Interracial problems will begin to surface. So long as the economy is going well, however, nobody's going to make a big fuss."

Democracy was likely to come eventually, in any case.

"You can hope. There are three camps developing in the PAP now: conservatives, liberals, and those in the middle who are undecided. I have some faith in Prime Minister Goh Chok Tong."

For some reason, that was comforting. Whom did Zulfikar speak for within the Muslim community?

"Let me put it this way: I spoke to a number of people about the *tudung* issue last year. Most signed our petition, although some did not. They were afraid. A culture of fear of the Internal Security Department exists in Singapore. People are afraid to talk. Myself, I don't mind irritating them. We are trying to end that culture. People send me e-mails in secret, but are afraid to respond openly. If I can make my views known openly, and I'm still here, then what is there to be afraid of? That's one thing that I'm trying to do. Also, many of these issues have been swept under the carpet, where they fester. I think we should air these issues, and solve them."

What about the leaders of his Muslim community, those who were in parliament?

How did the politicians become Muslim leaders, Zulfikar asked. "They are members of parliament who belong to the ruling People's Action Party. They are not elected by the Muslim community. I did not vote for them to be my leaders. If you are a Muslim or Malay leader, your role should be to take our grievances, our interests, to the parliament. That is not the case. What we see instead is that these people are bringing the government's policies to us. Their primary responsibility is to the PAP. How effective can they be when the Muslim community and the PAP's interests are in contradiction?" Malay-Muslims also needed their own independent community leaders, he said.

The first half of 2002 was a tumultuous period for Zulfikar. A newspaper article recounted that "the 30-year-old sales manager has transformed himself from a presence on the Internet into a man who is almost single-handedly taking on a government in the throes of remaking Singapore."[11] First, when he was interviewed by the BBC, Zulfikar criticized the government's support for the U.S. war on terrorism and said that Osama bin Laden was a better Muslim than the political leaders in parliament. In the furor that followed, he resigned as chief executive officer of fateha.com but continued to use his Web site to champion the *tudung* issue. He "waved the banner of cross-strait Islamic solidarity"[12] when he received two delegations from Malaysia's opposition fundamentalist Parti Islam SeMalaysia. He was later fined for refusing to leave a police station after an opposition politician was arrested, and finally, Zulfikar's computer was seized by authorities investigating whether he had criminally defamed Muslim Affairs Minister Yaacob Ibrahim and others in his postings on the Web site.

Then in late July, as events were building rapidly toward a climax, Zulfikar disappeared.

His wife and their four children crossed the border and went to her parents' house in Malaysia. Zulfikar himself later surfaced in Melbourne, Australia, where he told the media he knew what the outcome of the police investigation would be, and that the prospect of up to two years in jail had prompted his decision to flee. His family would soon join him, and he planned to continue to work for his cause.

"After stirring up the community, he flees to Australia," Yatiman Yusof said. "He should be honorable enough to stay behind and fight for what he believes and perceives as a right cause."[13]

I had to wonder if Zulfikar was as aware of his actions and their consequences as he portrayed himself to be. He was a likable fellow, charismatic and bright. It seemed, however, that he was trying to forge Singapore's Muslims into a separate psychological and political in-group, and that this effort was perceived as working at cross purposes with the government's intention to establish a Singaporean identity that transcended racial and ethnic groups. Lee Kuan Yew had labored for decades at bringing Singaporeans into an efficiently functioning economic and political whole. Zulfikar strove to pry Singapore's Muslims away as a religious and political faction perhaps more tightly connected to international Islam than to the nation. How such a development might affect the city-state's hyperdeveloped economy, which always faced difficulties of scale, could only be imagined, but it was probably safe to say that the result would not be positive. It was inevitable, especially in the post-September 11 political environment, that an anxious government would react against Zulfikar. How could he not have known this?

How could he not have known? The thought recurred as I sat in a light blue taxi winding along hills covered with low trees toward the Ministry for Muslim Affairs, a towering complex located away from the city center, to meet Minister Yaacob Ibrahim. His offices were spacious, simple, and functional. He was not a longtime politician, but a relative newcomer, trained as an engineer with a Ph.D. from Stanford University. Wearing slacks and a shirt open at the collar, he gestured to a couch and asked if I would like a cup of coffee.

Yaacob was not without a grin and an occasional burst of laughter, although it was obvious that his duties weighed on him. There was a comfortable feeling about the man, yet there remained a distance implied by his position, by its responsibilities and decisions affecting the lives of Singaporeans, particularly Muslims, and especially now. He seemed to be squeezed between the desires of his Malay-Muslim community and the needs of the government at a crucial moment in the nation's history. I asked if he found this a difficult time to be the minister for Muslim affairs.

Yaacob's face crinkled. He laughed aloud. "I might say it's difficult because I want to give some importance to my job, but it is difficult because we are coming to a point in the community where we are trying to grapple with certain issues and how those issues should be seen in the context of modern Singapore. We never expected these things, and the Malay community was not prepared."

What developments had not been anticipated?

"We didn't expect the *tudung* matter to be such a big issue. We've had requests in the past, one or two families, and schools had even allowed it on a case-by-case basis. But all of a sudden it became what it is. What we are really dealing with is the issue of pluralism. We've been in Singapore for the last thirty-seven years, never had any problem with this notion of Muslim identity vis-à-vis our national identity, and I don't think we have any problems now, in that we've evolved a lifestyle that gives us the opportunity to have our religious life and to be a part of modern Singapore. We have our mosques to do our daily prayers, we can go to Mecca to perform the haj every year if we can afford it, every fasting month we can go to do our prayers, and our kids can be sent to the mosque to receive religious instruction; yet at the same time, they have opportunities to learn about science and technology in the national mainstream schools."

What were the most important problems that Singapore's Malay-Muslim community faced today?

"The problem still remains a lack of education, because it is the key to all opportunities. Whether we like it or not, we still face some social problems. We make up most of the bottom 30 percent."

This was what I had read in the scholarly works on Singaporean society, although there seemed to be different reasons given for it. In Yaacob's opinion, why was this?

"I think to a large extent, many Malay families have not been able to overcome the cycle of poverty, which is passed on to the next generation."

Was that partly an effect of colonialism?

"Several books have been written that suggest the colonial policy of divide and rule did not benefit the Malays, and Malays at that time were only given opportunity for vernacular education. Malay access to English education came very late. After Singapore became independent in 1965, there was a huge debate about the future of Malay schools. Malays made a conscious effort to switch to English, the working language, because they realized that that was the way to move forward. We were starting from a low base, because not many of us were highly educated. You had a new nation that was racing forward, so it was a matter of trying to catch up. One hypothesis I have is that if you look at the 1970s, that was a time when social problems in the Malay community began to creep up: We had high numbers of drug addictions, and it was a time when women left home to work in factories and we suddenly had dual incomes, the family structure changed, and we couldn't adjust to the industrial state. Children dropped out of the educational system prematurely. However, at that time, at that stage of economic development of the country, there was enough work to absorb Malays into the labor force: We could work in factories, become dispatch riders, and so forth, but we cannot continue in that way today."

The great upheavals of the 1970s, it seemed, had been felt worldwide. Was Mendaki, the Muslim support organization, at least a partial solution to these educational and social problems?

"It started out right, which was to focus on education. I would like to ascribe the successes our community has enjoyed to the presence of Mendaki. We managed to plant the idea that education is important. You can see it now in every

Malay family, especially those who've been able to make it, that the next generation has an interest in education. Many low- and middle-income Malay families are spending a lot of money on education.

I told Yaacob that I had a young colleague who had been tutored by Mendaki and had gone on to do very well in university and now professionally as well.

"Good. I've redirected Mendaki, because I think we have to focus attention now on low-income families. Increasingly, I think the middle income and upper middle can take care of themselves. They're smart enough to find out where the opportunities are, but if you have a low-income family with both parents working, the situation becomes problematic if they have young children."

So you are trying to break the chains that have reached through generations?

"That's the whole idea. With our new Mendaki structure we are working with other partners as well. We work with mosques, community development councils, and community clubs. We go wherever we find low-income Malays and look at the local service providers, who can be Chinese, Indian, Malay—it doesn't matter. If there is a center that is offering tuition, and your son needs tuition, send him there. If you have a problem with finance, we'll step in. We'll help lower the barrier, but you must make the effort to get over it."

Singapore was small enough that he could accomplish some of these things. The Malay-Muslim community must be roughly 400,000 people.

"Yes, we have an advantage of size."

What did Yaacob think of the fateha.com Web site, which had prominently criticized him, I asked.

Yaacob laughed, not without a slight edge. "Should I give

an objective view?" He laughed again. "I respect the right of individuals to express their views. I always invite people to come to my office and discuss issues. I am, however, against people who demean that process and cast aspersions on it. I don't think that's the way to do things. You cross a certain line, and we have to come down hard on you. If you feel for example, that we are not effective, and your basis is factual, I can accept it. If your basis is that I'm not as good a Muslim as others, then I don't think that's right. We have to be careful about how the debate is conducted. I think we need to have a certain decorum and etiquette."

Did he think fateha.com lacked that?

"I leave that for you to judge."

I said that I had spoken with Zulfikar before he left Singapore, and one of his many objections seemed to be that Yaacob and others were not direct representatives of Muslims.

"We are not elected in terms of religious representation, but the government recognizes that within the political establishment there must be people who are able to speak for certain groups. There are members of parliament who represent the labor unions, and we have those who represent women's issues—they aren't elected by only women. It's a responsibility I was given, to deal with the Malay-Muslim community and help it to move forward. I accepted that responsibility. My colleagues and I have engaged in a process of consultation. We have met the religious elite and other community leaders. I think Zulfikar has it wrong. We seek feedback."

What were his thoughts when Zulfikar fled to Australia?

"I wasn't in Singapore. I was overseas when I found out. He claimed that he might be prosecuted and put in jail. I suppose it's his personal decision. Some people see it in a less-than-flattering light."

It was a deeply complicated situation, I thought, and it was connected with the wave of fundamentalist religion that had arisen amid the spread of modernity and rational, scientific thought. What was Yaacob's perception of Singapore's position within what was sometimes characterized as a global awakening of Islam?

"It is a historical phenomenon. Southeast Asian Muslims are also affected by events across the world. Wahhabism from Saudi Arabia has touched Indonesia and influenced us here in Singapore. Nowadays, with the Internet, things move fast. We are exposed to these influences. The question arises then, what is our response? I'm keen for the Malay community to reflect on this. I think we have to decide once and for all, what will our identity be in Singapore? My reply to that question is that we have already decided to become Singaporean. We have also decided that we want to be good Muslims and Malays as well. We want to have the best of everything, and we have that here. We can fulfill our religious life, and we can also fulfill whatever we desire for ourselves and our children in terms of development and technology. We have done this, so what's the problem? Well, someone comes in and says, 'You people are not practicing Islam correctly,' and we must be able to say they are wrong, we have got it right, don't tell us how to do it."

Yaacob's rationality was admirable. At the quiet center of powerful, conflicting forces, he remained calm and stable. The thought occurred that perhaps he brought an engineer's appreciation for motion, speed, and mass to the political currents that swirled around him. Why had the potential for conflicts between national and religious identity become such an issue these days, I asked.

"I think there are voices outside the community who feel that what we are doing so far is not Islamic. I beg to differ. It's not for them to judge. It's for God to judge."

What did he think of the idea of mixing religion and government, something that had spread lately to Indonesia, Malaysia, and throughout the region?

"My personal feeling about an Islamic state is that it is a new movement. If you look at the late nineteenth century, the idea wasn't to create an Islamic state, but for us to embrace Islam in its original form so that we could produce the scientists and thinkers and philosophers that we once did, to revitalize the glory of Islam. Somewhere during the twentieth century the political attitude shifted and it became necessary to have an Islamic state before you could do this. My view is that you do not need to have an Islamic state to have good Muslims. Also, while a certain amount of Islamic teaching is necessary to produce good Muslims, we also need to think about food, jobs, and economic success."

When the Jemaah Islamiyah terrorist suspects were arrested in Singapore, what was Yaacob's reaction? Was he surprised at the development?

"I was worried and angry. I hoped this was not a trend. I was also worried that such an event could cast doubt on our community. We needed to condemn them very quickly, we needed to distance ourselves from them, because if not, people would doubt us. Any such ideas are wrong. Killing innocent people is wrong."

What could possibly lead people with families and good jobs to commit acts of terrorism?

"I think they were misled, that perhaps they believed by doing something of that nature they were promised a place in heaven. You see, in any society, there are always people who believe in the idea similar to that of those seeking the millennium. These thirteen people tended to be a closed group, like a cult, not ordinary Singaporean Muslims. There was a central figure who was very charismatic and may have convinced them of the righteousness of his plans."

It was a pattern that was becoming predictable, I realized. At the center of each web was a militant cleric bringing believers under his spell, convincing them to hate outsiders, to slay the new "crusaders" from the modern world. The fear and dread oozing from the clerics was becoming comprehensible. The powers they exerted over other Muslims were threatened and eroded by the encroaching West, with its secular education, its seductive music, its suggestive movies and videos, its fast lifestyles, its freedoms. . . . Above all, they despised the freedoms.

TO BALI AND BACK

LATE 2002—GUNARATNA SAID THAT AFTER SINGAPORE'S INTER-
NAL SECURITY DEPARTMENT FOILED THE ATTACKS BY JEMAAH
ISLAMIYAH, THE GROUP'S OPERATIONAL COMMANDER, HAMBALI,
ANGRILY CALLED A MEETING IN SOUTHERN THAILAND, WHERE HE
RECONFIGURED THE STRATEGY FOR TERROR. Because they had
been disrupted to an extent that made it difficult to strike
well-defended installations in Singapore, he decided that
his men would go after easier prey—soft targets around
Southeast Asia where unsuspecting Western vacationers
could be found in abundance, gathering around the region's
many tourist resorts.

Tourist destinations had little security and were simple to
infiltrate, even with bulky explosives that had to be concealed
in vehicles or in backpacks, so at Hambali's orders, Jemaah
Islamiyah terrorists linked to the cleric Bashir and probably

funded by Osama bin Laden, struck on the Indonesian resort island of Bali, an artistic enclave with a predominantly Hindu culture, killing more than 200 people in a late-night attack on Kuta village discotheques with two bombs—one concealed in a vehicle and the other carried by a suicide bomber. Many who died were Australian rugby players in town for an annual tournament. News reports said that charred bodies were stacked up at the doors, where they had died in a struggle to claw their way from the inferno around them.

A week later, Indonesia finally passed antiterrorism laws. Within hours, police detained cleric Bashir, saying they wanted to question him about a plot to kill President Megawati Soekarnoputri and some previous bombings of Christian churches. Bashir checked into a hospital in Solo, near his school on the main island of Java, while squads of his jihadi followers clad in military garb clustered and stood watch outside. Nevertheless, he was subsequently removed to Jakarta and kept under police custody while evidence for various charges was compiled.

Two years earlier, we had visited Bali, staying in the mountains on the outskirts of Ubud at the Tjampuhan, a small hotel that had once been the home of Walter Spies, a German artist who had essentially transferred his knowledge of European-style painting to the Balinese, who had learned it effortlessly. Everyone in Bali seemed to pursue some form of art or craft, from painting to jewelry making, woodcarving and gamelan music to stone sculpture or dancing. It was a society that regarded artistic expression—much of it related to their Hindu religion—as a significant aspect of life. Our taxi driver told us that he participated in the *kecak*, a sweaty fire-dance production that featured a choir of chanters, trance states, curved kris swords, golden deer, and dancing on hot coals. It would be difficult to find a more fluidly expressive people anywhere in the world. Balinese dancing, in particular —with its reverberating gamelan music performed by orchestras before decaying stone temples—radiated a sensual charm that transcended the everyday world. Dancers wrapped in gleaming silk and gold swayed rhythmically against the night, burning the intense beauty of their images into your memory. We stayed for a week at the hotel, which is built along the verdant side of a small rainforest canyon with a swift, muddy-red river at the bottom. We did some sightseeing, bought a few paintings, and went each night to performances of various traditional dances, including the most graceful of them all, the *legong*. The week had passed quickly, like an enchantment, then we'd found ourselves back in Singapore, decompressing and getting reacquainted with our workaday lives.

This time it was different. We made another journey to Bali, but it felt as though we were under a threatening shadow. The terrorists' blasts and the conflagration that had consumed the lives of so many revelers had brought not only the world flooding in with it, but the worst part of the world: Islamists who were delighted to bring suffering and death to all. Bali was suffering. Tourism, the lifeblood of the island, had slumped abysmally. Balinese were taking home less money or losing their jobs. We checked into the Dynasty Hotel on Kuta beach, where the desk clerk said that Australians, who had formerly made up the bulk of their clientele, had simply stopped coming. There were more Singaporeans now, she said, because the national airline was featuring a special package for several months, but the occupancy rate was still only half of normal. The month after the bombing, tourist arrivals had fallen by more than 50 percent to their lowest level in about eleven years. It was a bitter time for the island.

Bali made $1.4 billion from tourism in 2001, a figure that was halved in the twelve months after the bombing. While I was having a massage by the pool, the masseuse told me she'd made 150,000 rupiah the preceding month, which was roughly $15. She had three children. I tipped her $10. Later in the evening, a taxi driver conveyed my wife, Miwa, and me well out of town to Batubulan for a *kecak* fire dance, where an ensemble of more than a hundred artists performed for thirty paying customers, which was sad because the dancers gave everything in their performance—a much livelier version than the one we had seen two years earlier.

Some Western purists I spoke with expressed their displeasure at the development of Bali and seemed to long for the island to regress into some imaginary primitive state. The desire for the Balinese to sink back into a more unspoiled condition was not shared, however, by the objects of their ostensible affections, the islanders themselves, who aspired to blend the modern offerings of the West with their traditional ways. Thus, owning a Toyota and being able to afford an occasional visit to Kentucky Fried Chicken were not seen by the Balinese as acts of cultural impurity, but as good things to be added to the mix, as were television sets, washing machines, and video games, which provided almost as much joy for the youngsters as cockfights, the national sport and a source of endless entertainment.

Could the act of bombing Balinese nightclubs frequented by Westerners be seen in some obscure way as an act of cultural purification? Some Europeans and Americans of liberal disposition and extremely tolerant natures seemed to suspect so, having been at least partially taken in by the very fanaticism of the terrorists, who are single-minded and harbor no doubts, while we Westerners are often assailed by them. We are often quite unsure of ourselves, having been taught tolerance, that cultures are not better or worse, but simply different and relative to one another. The terrorists have contempt for tolerance. They believe that they are right, and that the remaining tribes of humanity are infidels. They know that they will be called to paradise, and that the rest of us are doomed. No hidebound, redneck Mississippi Klansman was ever more prejudiced, or ever hated others more viciously. Islamism is a new totalitarianism that many of us in the developed West are ill prepared to cope with as we linger in what might be described as a state of privileged liberal guilt.

Miwa and I ate at a rickety pole-and-bamboo structure by the beach, where we chose fresh fish and prawns for grilling over a coconut-husk fire, sipped lime juice, and enjoyed warm breezes gusting in over a green, whitecapped sea. Some restaurant workers were preparing small wicker baskets of flowers for an offering to their gods at a local temple, which they did twice a day, said our pert, bespectacled waitress, who wore a red-and-white baseball cap. The Balinese are a deeply religious, friendly people who revere the arts, while the Wahhabi-influenced terrorists are "religious" only in their puritanical adherence to form, and are devoid of any real compassion for humanity. Wahhabis despise music and dance, and have been known to slay other Muslims for participating in either. If there was ever a clear example of good and evil, uncomplicated by mitigating factors, the Bali bombing was such a case. The predators had taken innocent lives, and in the aftermath of their attack, they had laughed and crowed about their happiness at its success.

The next morning, we went to visit the blast site, an enormous scar gouged out of the tourist-village landscape. The wound was healing, but it was still ugly. The two discos were gone, and the crater had been filled in so that there was a long vacant lot of about an acre, filled with bits of rubble and planted with a few small, forlorn palms. A sort of makeshift altar had been erected at the rear, where an elderly couple, perhaps the parents of an Australian rugby player who had passed on to other fields, wandered aimlessly. Nearby buildings were burned and skeletal, and across the street the Aloha Club was gutted and boarded up. A quiet solemnity still hung over the area, and after surveying it for a few minutes we left, walking toward the beach, pausing at shops to read the T-shirts on offer: One said, "Osama Don't Surf," a pun on the famous Robert Duvall line from the movie *Apocalypse Now*, which was rather clever; "Cry for Bali, October 12, 2002," which wasn't clever but seemed appropriate considering the number of tourists on the streets. I saw only two or three others, poking around the many open-air stalls where shopkeepers moped or slumbered, swatting at occasional flies in the heat. One T-shirt read simply, "Black Monday," and of course, there was a predictable but inspiringly defiant, "Fuck Terrorism, Vacation in Bali." I found an "Osama Don't Surf" in my size and bought it, as well as a Spiderman T-shirt for Emerson, who was back in Singapore and would be expecting gifts upon our return.

The owner of a small hotel near the beach said, "The terrorists really hurt us because all we have in Bali is tourism." Things were beginning to recover. In the weeks after the blast, his hotel had dropped to 5 percent occupancy but had crawled back to 40 percent or so. "We are much more aware of terrorism now," he said, adding grimly, "It won't happen again." And indeed, the investigation headed by a Balinese Hindu police general, I Made Pastika, had swiftly tracked down more than a score of terrorists involved in the bombing, many of them associated with the Wahhabist-influenced Islamist school on Java headed by Bashir, or linked to the cleric personally or through family ties. One of them, a forty-year-old mechanic named Amrozi, quickly became known as the "smiling bomber" because of the delight he displayed in court at having helped kill so many people, even when he was confronted by hideously burned and scarred Australians who had returned to testify against him. Amrozi, who was not from Bali but from Java, didn't like Americans, infidels, or white people. He was happy with his deeds and found it all quite amusing.

That night, we had dinner at a restaurant in the Dynasty Hotel, accompanied by a good little Balinese quintet—two acoustic guitars, a standup bass topped with a carved dragon's head, drums, and a fiddle. The bass player asked if we had any requests. I asked for anything by Bob Dylan. They flipped open a thick book of tunes and soon emerged with smiles, playing a fine version of the antiwar chestnut from the 1960s, "Blowin' in the Wind." The lyrics still bristled with relevance, but a melancholy thought occurred that wars have always been with us, and that particular song may continue to be meaningful for a long time to come.

I gradually became aware that the attacks of September 11, the war in Afghanistan, the jailing of Jemaah Islamiyah terrorists in Singapore—which was followed by a second roundup—and the bombing in Bali were transforming my notions about peace and war. I'd believed in peace at any cost since 1966, when, as a young sailor fresh out of boot camp, I'd suffered some serious injuries in an auto accident and was hospitalized with fellows who had been wounded in Vietnam and sent home. The ward housed broken jaws, which I had, and plastic surgeries, which most of the other guys, having been hurt much worse, were undergoing. Some of them were grotesque, faces blown apart, burned so their mothers wouldn't recognize them, multiple amputations of limbs. . . . Six weeks among them altered my beliefs. War did terrible things to good people, to those who were in many ways the finest and most devoted. Then a former football teammate who'd joined the Marine Corps was killed, the peace movement began, and in the last days of the 1960s when I was discharged, feeling psychologically traumatized and radicalized against a war that had taken some of the best of my generation, seemingly for nothing, San Francisco beckoned. Had the Vietnam War accomplished anything of obvious significance, perhaps that would have made it more understandable and acceptable. But as it was, those experiences built my foundational attitude against war that stood until September 11, 2001, when it began to crumble under the light of reconsideration.

Once again, things had changed.

Now, the dying innocents were victims not of imperialist U.S. government policies or a mistaken foreign adventure, but were being slain and maimed by religious fanatics. I thought of the passengers in hijacked airliners, people—including children—who had done nothing to harm the terrorists, who were only trying to get on with their lives like the rest of us. I remembered the workers in the twin towers. I considered the vacationers in the Bali discotheques who had died in the blast and fire. They may have been drinking and carrying on late into the night, but that was no crime. They hadn't been guilty of any heinous misdeeds or deserving of the painful deaths inflicted on them, except in the feverish brains of a band of deluded fanatics.

This created an uneasy tension with assumptions left unquestioned for decades. An internal scale that balanced idealism with realism—which had been more or less fixed in the 1960s and weighted heavily toward the former—began shifting toward the center. A political position that is firm for thirty years takes on a sense of permanency. An ironclad rigid concept such as "war is wrong" would never need to be questioned further. Those of us whose politics were forged in the crucible of Vietnam-era liberalism are perhaps prone to overlook the lessons of the previous war against German and Japanese totalitarianism because they were not learned through firsthand experience. We may also forget that perhaps the greatest liberal of all, President Franklin D. Roosevelt, was an effective and inspiring wartime leader. The rediscovery that armed conflict is not always morally wrong can strike the mental world like an earthquake, cascading through interlaced psychological networks in an unsettling series of adjustments, until life again comes into balance. Things had changed. Even the linguistic nuance of the word "liberal" may have shifted in the decades since the New Deal and the Great Society. Pulitzer Prize–winning writer Michael Skube argued that "most Americans, by now, understand that what is a conservative today was a liberal yesterday. Freedom of the individual today is an article of faith in the conservative catechism."[1] Freedom is what it has always been about.

In the aftermath of such a realization, it is no longer possible to be cocksure about the validity of sweeping concepts such as "war is wrong." There may eventually emerge a pale reassurance in taking the measure of events and gauging appropriate responses in a protean and threatening world where the most crucial priority is security.

Security may mean retaliation or even preemptive strikes to render impossible further attacks against the American people or their way of life, which in an interconnected sense may also mean attacks against international capitalism or peoples who form integral parts of the modern world economic systems upon which we all depend for our lives. Those systems have begun to seem more fragile as it has become necessary to defend them from terrorists. The airline and tourism industries, and those employed in them, for example, suffered gravely in the aftermath of the attacks. Hotels and airlines went bankrupt. Workers found themselves in the dole lines or on the streets. A former flight attendant, one among many in Singapore who had lost her job, mused glumly that she had "bin" laid off.

It had once seemed that there was a common desire for peace among all of the world's peoples. Now, that presumption had been shattered by a loosely organized army of terrorists dedicated to an ideology of hatred, trained and experienced in asymmetrical warfare, and looking to obtain weapons of mass destruction to kill as many of us as possible. Interestingly, the more liberal and tolerant our societies became, the more they hated us, because it was our very tolerance they despised, the quality that makes possible our pluralistic, free societies. The writer Paul Berman argued that Islamist terrorism is a continuation of a series of totalitarian responses against progressive modernity that began in the previous century with nazism and Japanese imperialism. He wrote of Islamism's influential theorist, Sayyid Qutb, whose "great purpose in life was to alert Muslims to understand that if tolerance and open-mindedness were accepted as social values, the new habits of mind would crowd out the divine. He wanted Muslims to remember that, in Islam, the divine is everything, or it is not divine. . . . God cannot be shunted into a corner."[2] Like nazism and Japanese imperialism before it, Islamism rejects the fragile growth of tolerance that is emerging in the modern world and seeks through force and violence to regress to the past to create a "utopian" totality. It is not desirable for different peoples to live together in peace; there must be an Islamist state and a regulated existence within it, which is precisely what the Taliban were creating in Afghanistan. While Berman may very well be right that Islamism is only the most recent in a series of fascist threats, it is new in our time, and it is changing the way in which we perceive the world, rousing us into a more pragmatic realism. It seems essential to awaken to the seriousness of the threat posed by terrorism, and still, there are phrases that ring softly in our memories, like echoes of John Lennon saying, "Give peace a chance," which is a good, even desirable view that will always make a strong claim. It may be inappropriate to accord it the highest priority amid a global assault by terrorists, but we can hope that such a time may come again.

Singapore, by virtue of its excellent security, had been spared a catastrophe like that on Bali. It has kept the terrorists at bay, although there is little doubt that Jemaah Islamiyah's leaders would dearly love to wreak havoc on the prosperous city-state if they could get off an attack, for symbolic as well as for strategic reasons. Singapore is the most Westernized and developed part of Southeast Asia, it has the closest ties with the United States, both commercial and security links, and it has an ethnic-Chinese majority that poses an obstacle to the terrorists' dream of creating an Islamist state throughout the region. In addition, the Muslim population of Singapore is moderate and has been to a significant extent mainstreamed into Singaporean society, although that integration is unfinished and still being carried out through the offices of Mendaki and by the larger policy aims of the government.

One man who had been observing the regional and global developments of militant Islamism with deep concern was the tough-minded senior minister of Singapore, Lee Kuan Yew, who at almost eighty years of age had no intention of allowing anyone to derail his ongoing accomplishment, which is building the nation that he had led for nearly four decades. On a drizzly afternoon about two months after the Bali attack, the senior minister's press secretary, Yeong Yoon Ying, showed me into his office in Istana Palace, an impressive and imposing piece of colonial architecture that has been beautifully preserved amid a wide, park-like setting. After chatting for a few moments about Japan and its problems, we turned our attention to Singapore.

"It's only thirty-plus years," Lee said. He wore an open-collar shirt and a dark cardigan sweater on a day that passed for chilly in the tropics. His white hair receded on the translucent dome of his forehead, and he spoke directly about the issues before him, no matter how complex or delicate. I felt that Lee was admirable not only for his plain speaking, but also for the things he had done to bring prosperity to his people, not all of those things easy or nice, but usually for the greater good, which was more than could be said for most politicians in Southeast Asia, or in other parts of the world for that matter. We still had race riots in the United States, which was also true of England and Germany and other developed multiethnic nations, but in Singapore race relations were not so bad. To begin with, the city-state has no ghettos.

"Ghettos are the most important problems," Lee said. "We had a chance when we rebuilt the city from 1965. Fundamental, was the rehousing of the people. We made sure there were no ethnic ghettos. There's no area where you enter and suddenly feel that it's bad, a depressed area, depressed shops, depressed restaurants. They breed self-pity and resentment. We made a conscious effort to make sure that people were mixed. In other words, your neighbors are mixed, your children's schools are mixed, you have shops that are mixed. And it's only recently that this *halal* business, of not having somebody consume non-*halal* food near you has become an issue. For all my years, in the 1970s, 1980s, even in the 1990s, I sat down with my Muslim fellow students, fellow MPs, or constituents, they ate their food and I ate my food. That makes for an easy relationship. Now, with the resurgence of Islamic orthodoxy, strict observance of Islamic diet codes, behavior codes, dress, et cetera, there is a certain divide. This is part of a worldwide problem and we have to live with it."

How far-reaching were the effects of the September 11 and attempted Jemaah Islamiyah terrorist attacks on Singapore, and had ethnic relations been significantly altered?

"The threat is a long-term one. It gave early warning that

the terrorists can succeed despite all the precautions we take. Given the nature of our population, supposing they'd succeeded in exploding a bomb at the Yishun train station; they would have killed Muslims besides American sailors, but they would also have killed many Chinese and Indians. That would not have been helpful for race relations. The warning was that we had to be prepared, because it can happen despite all precautions. They are invisible, their bomb-making capacity has been disseminated among hundreds of people who've gone through their training camps. While ammonium nitrate is bulky, other explosives are not. That's a problem."

But had it affected ethnic relations in Singapore?

"Not yet, because no bomb has gone off. But it will if a bomb does go off and kills not just Americans, British, Australians, or Israelis, but also Chinese, Indians, and Malay-Muslims. You're dealing with people in a mass. Who caused it? Muslims. Why? Because they are fighting to create a Muslim state in Southeast Asia."

It seemed that there was a desire in some circles to establish an Islamist state in Southeast Asia. From what possible problems or causes did he see this desire arising, and was this a threat to a nation like Singapore, with a minority Muslim population?

"No, I don't think it's a threat to Singapore. It's a threat to secular governments in Malaysia, Indonesia, and the Philippines. It's a nonachievable ambition but the call resonates. Let's say the Muslim radicals in Malaysia capture power. Are they going to surrender their power to Muslims in Indonesia or the Muslims in the Philippines? Why should they do that? These are clarion calls that resonate but have no basis in probabilities."

How did such threats arise, and how was Singapore to defend itself and its values against them?

"This is part of a worldwide surge. It's amazing how the same phenomenon has taken place in countries far apart. In Mauritius, for example, the prime minister who came through recently saw my prime minister. He said in the past ten years, 18 percent of his people who are Muslims, from India originally, have all gone separate. They eat differently and they have become distinct and separate, all in the past ten years. With Saudi money, they had mosques and religious schools built. It is worldwide. Over the past thirty years since the oil price quadrupled in 1973, petrodollars paid for the mosque-building, *madrassa* building, and the dispatching of *ulemas*, or preachers, to proselytize around the world. This has raised their religiosity, a feeling that Muslims are all one and ought to support each other. There is now an identification of these different and disparate Muslim groups with the Arab cause."

It had become a virulent strain, this new Wahhabist-influenced Islamism.

"It is. I don't know how long it will last, but it does no good."

Did he view the Jemaah Islamiyah detainees in Singapore as a result of problems in this country, or were they a product of the worldwide movement?

"It has nothing to do with us. They were studied by a group of psychologists and psychiatrists. Their actions had nothing to do with local conditions. They were found to be people who are easily taken up by these causes. They've been worked up. They want a cause, and the leaders captured them and dragged them along. And they feel that they are part of a great clandestine enterprise and, therefore, important. Secretly sending messages to each other, gathering money, collecting equipment to make a bomb to blast somebody, and if they die, they will go to heaven."

The white paper sounded interesting and I hoped to obtain a copy of it. Did Lee have an opinion about the fateha.com Web site and Zulfikar, who had gone to Australia?

"He is just a product of this whole surge. He's riding the surf to make himself important. Does he believe in it? Does he practice it? No. But does it make him feel important? Yes. Is he prepared to take the rap? No. So he scoots when his position is exposed. But others are prepared to take the rap. They are prepared to go to the end of the road. They are different people. So fateha.com is an irrelevance, but Jemaah Islamiyah, they are not irrelevant."

Lee had been quoted several times in the past, saying that Western-style democracy required certain conditions to function effectively, and that those may not have been met in Singapore. What were some of the conditions that would need to be met, and did he think they could be accomplished in his country?

"First, you've got to have an educated population. If you don't have an educated population, it's difficult to run a one man-one vote system. Look at some of the countries that have attempted it, and see the swings of the pendulum when there is no informed choice. Having an educated population takes time, time to develop a fairly sizable middle class well above the poverty line, time to reflect on the virtues of civic society, and issues of governance. Eventually they will form a stable base. When I was an undergraduate at Cambridge law school studying British Constitutional Law after the war, my lecturer, the professor, had been a cabinet secretary during the war. One day, I think it was 1947–48, he came in and said, 'There's the fifth change of government in Paris. The Latins are different temperamentally from Anglo-Saxons. We are pragmatic. Having taken the vote, we live with the consequences for the next five years and persuade the people to go our way after that. But not so with the Latins. Having lost, they immediately begin the fight to bring the government down.' In England, it was all done peacefully. I'm not sure you can do that without a large middle class accustomed to peaceful adjustment, accommodation, and change. Will we get to this stage? Yes, I think so, provided we don't run into setbacks. Are we certain to get there? I would say probably, but the accentuation of this Muslim distinctiveness will make it a more complicated enterprise. The voting will not be influenced by economic or social programs, but by religious biases."

Could Lee imagine liberal and conservative wings developing within the People's Action Party (PAP)?

"They are already there," the senior minister said, with something like comic exasperation. "Always have been. We occupy a unique position. A small island not intended to be independent became independent. Its choices are limitless in self-destruction, but most limited in the way it can move upward. We don't have all those luxurious options between cradle-to-grave welfareism and outright capitalism, freewheeling."

Was he saying that the tolerances between what was possible and what was necessary were narrower in a city-state of only 3 million citizens?

"We've got limited choices for progress, but unlimited for self-destruction. I think that's one reason why there has been one-party dominance. People complain, they grumble. We are developing a chattering class. But can they persuade the people to vote against the PAP? At the end of the day, they need a government that maintains peaceful conditions in Singapore, that provides jobs and prosperity and can stand up and not be beaten down by tough-talking neighbors. There's a limited number of people who can do that."

How would a more democratic society, if Singapore managed to get to that point, affect the racial harmony that had been achieved?

"Will we get there in spite of the racial divide? Probably yes, if we are able to develop a fairly considerable Malay-Muslim middle class that will not be influenced by religious considerations when voting. At the moment, the middle class is small. The lower middle class is large and the working class is larger than the lower middle class. It's a different social economic configuration."

How did he foresee Singapore changing in the next twenty years? Did he have a vision of what transformations might occur?

"It's not possible. Twenty years ago, could I have foreseen where we are today? No, because I could not foresee the development of information technology. I couldn't foresee how communications and transportation would change production patterns and make for this globalized marketplace. We have got to keep adjusting to a changing global environment."

He seemed to be perpetually involved in remaking Singapore.

"More at some times than others; at times you come to a critical turning point. Take a simple thing like communications cable. We commanded an important junction because the British laid the cables throughout the British Empire and on to Japan and America and so on and the cables went through

Singapore. The day they put up the satellite, that day our monopoly or dominance was threatened. So we had to go into satellite. But the day fiber optics came in for broadband and we laid fiber-optic cables in Singapore, that partially restored our position because the satellite cannot be as fast or as secure. So we are always moving with the technology and the way trade, industry, and economic activity change as a result of technology. Our problem is how do we—in the context of an Asia-Pacific where U.S. dominance has given us the stability and security plus the technology, trade, and industry and therefore allowed our growth—make these adjustments when gradually over the decades that dominance will not be so overpowering? This will have fundamental consequences. Will America and Japan, in alliance, maintain a balance with China? How do we in ASEAN [Association of Southeast Asian Nations] position ourselves? These are imponderables. The best outcome would be for ASEAN nations to be linked up to both America and Japan and also maintain good relations with China. Is that possible?"

You could only hope that it was.

"It is our business to try and navigate a course which offers us maximum space."

They had done well in their business thus far.

"But that does not mean we will continue to do so. The tide was with us. The wind was behind us."

But they had done well.

Lee's voice took on a deeper timbre, as though he was trying to impart something of significance. "We worked hard," he said, his voice shaking.

I shook the senior minister's hand at the door of his office. He was frail now, his skin was wrinkled and what hair remained was thin and white. I recalled the photos in his autobiography of a vigorous, handsome young labor lawyer-turned-politician with a full head of dark hair, rallying Singaporeans, working to create an independent nation. Time changes everything. Outside, the drizzle had quickly ceased, as it often does in the tropics. It was warm; there was a fresh smell and a light mist rising from the green, tree-lined fields around Istana.

About a week later, the white paper that Lee Kuan Yew had mentioned arrived on my desk. Titled "The Jemaah Islamiyah Arrests and the Threat of Terrorism," it was fifty pages long, and the section devoted to psychological profiling offered a starting point for attempting to understand why these Singaporean men were willing to kill innocent people and perhaps die themselves. What had stirred the rage in their hearts, sparked the homicidal gleam in their eyes? How had a group of men who had grown up in prosperous, quietly efficient Singapore become so radicalized that they were willing, even eager, to inflict incomprehensible suffering and death on ordinary people they didn't know?

As I went through the pages of the report, clues began to emerge. These men were not simple. They did not lack in education or in steady jobs and incomes. Of thirty-one total detainees from two roundups, all except two had average or above-average intelligence, and two had clearly superior minds. All of them had received secular educations—it wasn't as if they had been brainwashed as youths in the *madrassas* of Pakistan, as in the case of the Taliban—so it had been later in their lives that they had come to their collective radicalized state of mind. This had happened during a period of purposeful indoctrination that was performed cynically, and which bore similarities to the way devotees are recruited into religious cults. Jemaah Islamiyah utilized special handlers for this, professionals who were familiar with the mental weaknesses they could exploit and with psychological leverages they could use to manipulate their selected subjects, who had already displayed some initial willingness to go down this path for their cause.

In a typical Jemaah Islamiyah seduction, the first stage would be religious classes for a general Muslim audience, in which potential recruits could be identified as those who wished to know more about the plight of members of their religion in trouble spots around the world such as Bosnia, Mindanao in the Philippines, Indonesia's Malukus, or the Middle East. Jemaah Islamiyah's spiritual teacher, Ibrahim Maidin, would then seek to further arouse their emotions regarding these causes, and finally, within a year or two, when he felt personally sure about them, extend an invitation to join his group. Those selected for membership were infused with a sense of belonging to a superior in-group that was close to God by virtue of possessing the truth. All outsiders were demonized, even those who were Muslims but failed to subscribe to their particular set of violent, extremist values. An important principle they were taught and accepted, the psychologists noted, was that innocent non-Muslims and Muslims alike could legitimately be slain to accomplish the aims of their jihad.

To bind the Jemaah Islamiyah members more tightly to the group and persuade them to perform risky and violent acts, various manipulations were utilized, including pledges and psychological contracting. Maidin would stir his followers up with a barn-burner of a sermon, for example, then pass out surveys asking the members to respond with various actions they were willing to take, all the way up to sacrificing their lives. These documents were considered binding contracts that could not be changed later, even after the fiery emotions of the moment had died back to ashes. The status of martyrdom was promised to those who met their deaths in jihad, of course, with all the trappings of immediate paradise that entailed. This was a big payoff in the minds of the jihadis, and it was very easy for the clerics to guarantee that heaven awaited them.

The members, who may have come to Jemaah Islamiyah (JI) for any number of reasons initially, were thus persuaded that they had found a direct pathway to heaven and to God, as well as freedom from the daily stresses of maintaining a rational mind. There would be no further need to question or to search for the truth, as they had found it. "They believed they could do no wrong, as the JI leaders had quoted from holy texts. The psychological profile of JI members (e.g., high compliance, low assertiveness, low in the questioning of religious values, and high levels of guilt and loneliness) suggested that the group of JI members was pre-disposed to indoctrination and control by JI leaders and needed a sense of belonging without close attachments."[3] By the time the terrorists were instructed to carry out attacks, they had been trained to respond without question.

Terrorists can be seen as the most fanatical of murderers, which they are, but in light of the cult-style recruitment techniques employed to lure members into the fold and indoctrinate them into acting on behalf of a militant group, perhaps some of them can also be seen at least partially as victims themselves. Such a perspective occurred while riding up an elevator in a skyscraper in Singapore's financial district to a high-powered law firm to meet Subhas Anandan—a lawyer renowned for his championing of unpopular causes—who had decided to represent a Jemaah Islamiyah detainee who had been trained by the Taliban in Afghanistan and who had subsequently taken videos used to plan bombing attacks in Singapore.

The man in question was Mohamed Nazir, a Singaporean Indian with long flowing hair and a trimmed beard who stood out among the newspaper pictures of the detainees because he looked much like the hippie next door. His legal representative, Anandan, was also a Singaporean Indian, but a Hindu with a pompadour hairstyle, and as might be expected, an articulate manner of speaking. I told him that I had been working on a book about racial and religious harmony in Singapore when the September 11 attacks occurred, and that I had continued to observe and write, as the suicide attacks, the subsequent arrests in Singapore, and the bombing in Bali had put stresses on the social structure of his country that I hadn't expected in the early stages of my project.

He said racial harmony was something they talked about more in Singapore these days, as they tried harder to understand each other's religions. "There are new attempts being made to understand the Hindus," Anandan said, "and for the Hindus to understand the Taoists and the Buddhists and the Muslims. Well, it only goes to show one thing: The so-called racial harmony that we talk about, we should just call it religious tolerance. There is not something called 'harmony.' If there was real harmony, we wouldn't have to get excited about these sorts of things."

The economic situations Singaporeans found themselves in, relative to the rest of the Southeast Asian region, or indeed compared with global standards, were fairly good.

That, Anandan agreed, made it easier to tolerate each other, but still, harmony would be something different, something higher. Singaporeans knew they must tolerate each other or they wouldn't survive. "We are such a small country that if there isn't a high degree of tolerance of each other's religions and races, we would all sink. Singaporeans are smart enough to realize that we need to work together. We need each other to survive."

When you looked around the world, even that basic assumption of mutual need that had been made by Singaporeans may be better than the sorry states of racial relations that had been reached in many countries.

"Sure. If you compare what we have done with, even Malaysia, Indonesia, the Philippines . . ."

Even in some sense, the United States . . .

"Yes, even in the United States you have enduring racial problems, not so much religion, but with the whites, the blacks, the browns, whatever. . . . When we compare Singapore with all these countries, we are definitely on a higher plateau."

It could not be denied, he went on, that Singapore had created a better quality of tolerance, but still, harmony was something that Singaporeans had not yet achieved. "I hope that we will. I think the leaders of each of the communities are working toward that. One day we may reach the level where we can say, 'There is religious harmony.' We have to. We have no choice, actually."

Singapore was setting a pretty good example for other

countries in that way, both in its pragmatism and its progress, and in that light, I wondered, would it be possible to talk about Anandan's client, the Jemaah Islamiyah detainee, Mohamed Nazir?

He could talk about Nazir without infringing on his rights or privileges, because the jihadi had given instructions that his legal counsel could go public about his case and his plight. "His family came to me because I have a reputation of handling a lot of unusual cases. I suppose they thought that I might be able to help him. I went to see the parents, then I went to see this guy in jail. I asked why he did these things and found out that he was indeed a follower, that he was interested in learning the Koran, and because he was not good in Arabic or Bahasa Malaysia, he had to learn in English. This guru, Ibrahim Maidin, started teaching Nazir and others the Koran, and some of the students were kept after class, where he would tell them that their Muslim brothers were being oppressed, that the cause of this was the United States and Israel, and they had to fight them. He taught them that Osama was doing a good job, that he was the champion for this cause, and then some of them, including my client, went to Afghanistan."

Nazir had received training and further indoctrination in Afghanistan, the lawyer said, among al Qaeda and the Taliban. He returned to Singapore, and Jemaah Islamiyah decided to bomb strategic points such as the American embassy, the British embassy, and a mass transport station.

Had he admitted who made those decisions?

"The direction came from their leader, the guru, Maidin. Who gave Maidin his orders, my client doesn't know. He knows that his immediate leader is the one. They ordered the fertilizer so they could make bombs from it. Would they have done it? I think so. They would have carried out the instructions."

They were trying to get twenty-one tons of ammonium nitrate fertilizer to make explosives, the papers had reported.

"They didn't get so much though. They hadn't even figured out where to store it. I think they would have just kept it in the containers. I think they only secured a portion of that."

The papers said they had obtained about four tons of the fertilizer, which they wanted to smuggle into Singapore. Had Mohamed Nazir really seen things differently since he was apprehended, had he come back to reality after all this?

That was something only time would tell. "When you are brainwashed, they tell you to do this and do that. I think my client did not understand the larger picture, did not know what kind of harm he would do even to his Muslim brothers. When it was explained to him what would have happened, I think he began to see. Those who were actually sympathetic to your cause might have begun to hate you. Those people might have turned against you also. I don't think he realized all these things."

Still, Nazir was an intelligent man, in Anandan's estimation. "He was given tests and is in the top 20 percent of the population. He's no fool. But I think that if you don't agree with the hypnotist, it will be very difficult to hypnotize you. So I think my client also had some similar feelings, and that's why it was easy to control him. They were not resisting that much. There was some inherent sympathy."

And it was their sympathy for this Islamist cause that kept them from looking beyond it at the pain and confusion they would have caused?

"That's right."

Would he be detained for two years?

"He can be detained for two years, four, six, it can go on indefinitely under the Internal Security Act. If the authorities feel that the detainees have reformed, that they are sufficiently rehabilitated, they can be released before two years. But I don't think in this particular case that will happen." There was a possibility that he would be kept for two years or slightly more, then he might be released under restrictive orders. "He says he wants to go back to school. He already asked the detention body if he can do some courses, which he may be able to do, not this year, but next. I hope he does it, because he's quite a smart chap. He's too intelligent a fellow to be wasted."

Was Nazir cooperating with the authorities and telling them what he knew about the activities of Jemaah Islamiyah and al Qaeda?

He had told the Internal Security Division (ISD) everything that he knew. In that sense he had shown remorse and some good qualities in that he had not hidden anything. "He wouldn't know much, but I think that everything he knows, he has shared. My instruction to him was that if you want to enjoy an early release, then I think that you should cooperate with the authorities and convince them that you are on the right track. If you try to mislead them with the wrong information, that would be a sign that you were not rehabilitated."

Did the lawyer see him often?

"No, just before court appearances generally. Every time I see him, I send him a bill, and I think he's worried about that too." Anandan smiled and arched a bushy eyebrow. Lawyers, it seemed, were pretty much the same everywhere. Did the detainees know about the Bali bombing that followed their unsuccessful attempt to attack Singapore?

"I don't know. Maybe they do, because they may well be questioned about whether they knew it was on the agenda."

Were any of the others cooperating?

"I believe that most of them are, that they have confessed to many things. The ISD has confronted them with black-and-white evidence, so I think there is not much for them to deny. I may be wrong, but from what I can gather, there were a lot of admissions." And now, people in Singapore were growing worried, because they think they may be the next target.

Singapore had already been a target.

"Yes, but we are quite pro-American in our political stance, so they may try again. If they are able to place a bomb in a department store in Singapore, how many would die? If their aim is to create anxiety and fear, they are succeeding."

Yes, in that sense, perhaps they are.

"It's a lot of psychological manipulation. It's a pity. I am a Hindu. My twelve-year-old son asked me why people were always talking about the bad Muslims and the problems. I told him it wasn't a Muslim problem, that there were bad Hindus, Buddhists, and Christians. I don't want him and his generation to grow up thinking that Muslims are bad."

What could we learn from all this?

"I don't know, but I'll say this: Only in Singapore can a Muslim terrorist be represented by a Hindu who is the head of his own temple, and his law firm has a Jew as the senior partner."

We both laughed. That was very likely true.

What did he think of Yaacob Ibrahim, the current minister for Muslim affairs, and of the criticism leveled against him by Zulfikar Mohamad of the fateha.com Web site?

Singapore had the right man for the job in Yaacob Ibrahim, Anandan said. "His brother is also a partner in this law firm, by the way, but not just because of that. Yaacob has a very difficult task before him, and he's doing a fine job. Zulfikar may have some points, but he loses credibility through his unfair criticisms, many of which are not very rational. If he were more rational, he would have been more accepted. He should have tested his ideas in court. We could have settled it once and for all. I have defended dissidents, and this country has enough legal mechanisms to account for them and their causes."

Some months later, a Singaporean political writer who was also a Muslim said a similar thing, that Zulfikar had not gone too far, and that he should have fought his case in court. I had no way of knowing whether that was true, but as Zulfikar had a wife and four children to look after, Australia seemed like it might be a comfortable place for the activist to relax for a spell, reassess his life, and decide what to do with the rest of it.

In the aftermath of September 11, a mental health professional wrote an essay arguing that the inability of Middle Eastern peoples to develop democracies and to enjoy the freedoms and economic development associated with Western nations may have led to feelings of inferiority that were unbearably frustrating for certain Muslims who believed fervently that their devotion should guarantee blessings flowed to them from God.

Jungian psychiatrist Hechmi Dhaoui, who is from the Arab-Muslim world, suggested that Muslims' longing for the golden age of Islam was a form of compensation for a collective inferiority complex. This, he said, had created a situation in which it would be healthier to simply let go of the past, to sacrifice their nostalgic longing for a time they had never known except in fabulous tales of a distant, bygone age that faded from actual view centuries ago.

He asked that the United States "understand and help the Arab Muslim world in its effort to abandon this regressive attitude and to re-emerge in history. It is necessary that the United States assume their responsibility since they are politically and financially the ally of Saudi Arabia, which is the source of Islamism."[4] This proposition seemed to capture an intricate, multifaceted situation—through an unusual grasp of Arab psychology and political acumen—and outline a moral obligation of the United States. Wahhabist Islam had been growing in a sort of cultural petri dish in a hothouse provided by American money and political power that allowed the Saudis by virtue of the oil under their desert to avoid entering the modern world, and further enabled them to create a school of religious intolerance that they exported to far-flung parts of the world until it finally targeted the United States, the very source of their affluence, as the primary modernizer of the world and therefore their sworn enemy. This formulation bore an almost Shakespearean sense of tragedy.

Dhaoui argued that the secular ideology of Arab nationalism—which along with anti-Semitism was largely inherited from German National Socialism (nazism) and championed in the 1960s by Egypt's Gamal Abdel Nasser—had threatened the Saudi government and helped create a fear that led to its extensive financing of Islamism on a global scale. Saudi Islamists also held the Nasserites responsible for the humiliating loss to Israel in the Six Day War, which triggered a collective Arab memory of the loss of Andalusia, or southern Spain, an event that had precipitated their exit from history more than five hundred years earlier. Since that time, Dhaoui said, Middle Eastern Muslims had been searching for a way to participate meaningfully in global affairs, but their regressive governments had not allowed this, nor had they allowed democracy to develop.

The major reason for the lack of political development was a tradition of oppressive regimes throughout the region, where dictators of one stripe or another had long been the norm. Their active repression of political rights and of any sign of nascent civil society had allowed religious fundamentalism to flourish in the shadows and grow almost unnoticed until it flowered into violent Islamism.

The governments in question had often encouraged Islamists to blame the prosperous "infidel" West, especially the United States, for their problems of poverty and need, adroitly shifting responsibility away from the regimes that kept their citizens under the boot. U.S. support for Israel and an inability to solve the Palestinian problem was also a focus for Arab hatred that aided in the imposition of religious fascism. Islamists "would persuade Muslims to put away individual claims and to integrate themselves into the community of believers according to an old model, nostalgically revitalized without being spiritually authentic. This is, in fact, a way of preventing the Muslim world from progressing."[5] The Islamists thus "remain in a state of self-satisfaction that is at the edge of psychosis. They consider themselves as eternal victims without wondering about the reality."[6] Bound up in a state of absolute belief, Islamists are incapable of self-evaluation or criticism, because to engage in such activities would be heretical, and so once they have entered into this trap of fanaticism, the door slams shut and there is no available exit, no way other than jihad and martyrdom, or living a life of constant frustration and rage at their perceived victimization, made even more unbearable by the towering injustice of it all in light of what they regard as their unyielding faith. There was something terribly wrong with such a spiritual world, but the terrorists were not equipped to seek out the actual problems that bedeviled them because their extreme interpretations of faith could not be questioned.

Dhaoui's final analysis of the personalities of the terrorists allowed that while they considered paradise to be lost, it was still their rightful reward, and they could reclaim it through unquestioning belief and following the orders of God as relayed through their clerics. "The personality structure of the fanatic lacks suppleness; it is rigid with strong convictions based on false judgments. The fanatic's objective is merely to use others in order to gain entry to paradise by whatever means, including terrorism and murder. Fanatics are even capable of rejoicing when they inflict pain and harm on the other."[7]

This had led the analyst to conclude that Islam in its extreme form must learn to control irrational violence if it would return to the current of progressive history, much as individuals must learn to ameliorate their pathologically aggressive tendencies or be dealt with by society. To achieve this, he urged an end of Muslim nostalgia for its legendary past, followed by reentry into the history of humanity, reintegration into the world of what Islamists unfortunately regard as that of the infidel. He offered his Muslim brothers a key to this door, which is the insight that the other will be "different from us and still worthy of respect."[8] While Qutb would have disagreed with this, it is a crucial lesson and a self-evident truth that has emerged quite naturally in Singapore out of economic necessity.

MALAYSIA and IRAQ

EARLY 2003—AS WE PREPARED TO LEAVE SINGAPORE AND DRIVE
UP THROUGH MALAYSIA TO NORTHERN KELANTAN STATE TO INTER-
VIEW NIK AZIZ, LEADER OF PARTI ISLAM SEMALAYSIA (PAS), CON-
FRONTATION IN IRAQ WAS DRAWING NEAR. There was more at stake
than disarming a regime that had killed a million people and
had already used weapons of mass destruction, although this
seemed as though it should be enough. There was also the
aim of bringing change to the Middle East, including to the
heart and source of Islamist terrorism, Saudi Arabia. "A successful war in Iraq . . . would embolden those who wish for
the Arab world deliverance from retrogression and political
decay."[1] I wondered if this were possible, and could only
hope that it was.

A United Nations–sponsored study by Middle Eastern intellectuals called the *Arab Human Development Report 2002*

showed that the region was stagnating and falling further behind the developing world. Its low educational and income levels and repression of women stemmed largely from oppressive governments that did little to enhance the lives of their peoples and shifted the blame for their impoverished lives and frustrations to the United States, which had resulted in rampant anti-Americanism. The region had become a breeding ground for terrorists under its current regimes but possibly through intervention that could be improved. "The fundamental choice is whether the region's trajectory in history will remain characterized by inertia . . . or whether prospects will emerge for an Arab renaissance that will build a prosperous future."[2]

There was hope that replacing Iraq's regime—which under Saddam Hussein had become what the writer Robert D. Kaplan referred to as a "bureaucratic killing machine"[3] that fed off the country's oil revenue—with a democratic government would serve as a positive example for Middle Eastern peoples. To conceive of such a plan was bold, and to attempt to implement it ambitious on a scale with the successful struggle to contain communism, which had required the better part of five decades. Now, the administration of President George W. Bush, a particularly inarticulate leader, was proposing something on a similar scale. Bush had been placed largely through family connections in a position of immense power, and now it was demanded that he rise to a historical challenge the likes of which had not been seen since the time of Roosevelt. It seemed almost too much to ask, but there was little choice because the Islamist assault "that began in the Arab world spread to other shores, with the United States itself the principal target."[4] No president placed in that situation could remain passive. The difficulty would be in responding effectively.

We left Singapore by taxi, drove across the causeway to Johor Bahru and picked up a rented car with Malaysian plates, which I had been told were good for driving through small towns and speed traps, especially since there was an old rivalry between the two countries that had reemerged as a dispute over prices paid for water Malaysia supplied to Singapore. We cruised up the expressway through palm oil plantations toward Kuala Lumpur, Miwa in front and Emerson in back, covering the distance in about four hours, staying that night at the Mandarin Oriental Hotel, next to the Petronas Twin Towers, the tallest buildings in the world. We watched television coverage of a summit meeting of coalition leaders in the Azores. It was only a matter of days before conflict would break out. Saddam warned that such a war could spread beyond the region, in a less-than-veiled threat of terror attacks on civilians.

The next morning, we set out for the east coast of Peninsular Malaysia, winding up a small highway over the highlands that ran through the country's middle, where strange plants grew in the high altitude, spreading tree ferns, palms with long fronds and towering bamboo that draped over the narrow road. We stopped once and a curious monkey approached the car, raising up and peering in the window as Emerson squealed with delight. Then we were descending the mountains, swooping past lumber mills and plantations toward Kuantan, a town dominated by a great, blue-domed mosque and edged by a turquoise sea under clear skies. We turned north and wound along a white-sand coast in Terengganu state, staying a night at Tanjong Jara, a Malay-style resort run by a friendly Swiss, Peter Bucher, who had been in Southeast Asia for about thirty years.

Amid the rising political tensions, I asked how his business had been. He said it wasn't bad, but it would be nice to see an end to this Middle East thing. I had to agree. We settled in at a villa built almost entirely of local hardwood, a type of teak, with a wide veranda that offered a panorama of the South China Sea, and as evening descended, the sounds of waves and night birds, and the touch of warm breezes.

The next morning we awoke early for the drive to Kelantan state, turning on the television briefly to see Secretary of State Colin Powell announce that the United States would go it alone against Saddam with a small coalition of the willing. A wave of nearly physical anxiety came over me, composed mostly of hope for those about to go into battle, and sorrow for those about to die, to be maimed and suffer the havoc of war. I hoped that history would later prove the worth of what was about to happen, that the larger course of human events would bear out the necessity of the suffering that was about to take place.

After breakfast, we sped northward for Kota Baru, which was just below the border with Thailand. It was about a four-hour drive, Peter had told us when we left the resort. We sped easily along for a couple hours up a two-lane highway parallel to a placid blue sea, through a town with a single, green-domed mosque and colorfully painted cottages built on stilts, when we were flagged over, along with five or six other cars, by a uniformed police officer who wore dark glasses and spoke little English. All the cars pulled over and lined up at the roadside had been speeding, I was given to understand, and we had to pay a fine to a "politician" seated at a table, who was noting the fines in a large book and accepting cash on the spot.

How much?

My fine would be 300 ringgit, or about US$75, the police officer said. He asked what my profession was.

I was a journalist on my way to interview Nik Aziz, I replied, looking at my watch in the hope that this would take no longer than necessary.

The officer took me aside and said the fine would be only 50 ringgit, and that I should get on my way.

After handing over the money, I thanked him. We had all been driving faster than the posted speed limit. I wondered why he had decided to send me along with a reduced fine.

We soon reached Kota Baru, a jumbled city of mostly unattractive and dingy low buildings, and checked into the Renaissance Hotel, which was in the tallest, and most modern-looking building in sight. Nearly all the women on the streets were covered with the *tudung*, a head scarf, and flowing robes, which presented a uniform and pleasant appearance. There was some time to spare, so after showering and changing clothes, we relaxed, turned on the television and watched President Bush issue a forty-eight hour ultimatum for Saddam and his sons to leave Iraq. There *was* a certain "cowboy" quality about the president from Texas, and maybe that was not a completely bad thing, given that the world had been plunged once again into circumstances that bore such obvious metaphorical resemblances to the Old West. Still, the domestic policies of the younger Bush, his tax cuts, swelling budget deficits, and lack of jobs creation, were pure, warmed-over voodoo economics. War was almost inevitable now. My appointment with Aziz was for two o'clock.

A well-groomed desk clerk said he would call a taxi that would take me to the house of the Tok Guru, which was known to everyone, and a cab, looking somewhat battered, nevertheless arrived promptly. The driver, who was rail-thin with hair swooped back over his ears, said his name was Ramli. He wore dark glasses and rock music blared from his radio. He looked to be about forty and seemed like a decent, friendly sort. The air conditioner wasn't working, he said, so all the windows were rolled down. It was steaming hot. I asked him about Aziz.

"He's a good man, I think," Ramli said, glancing back over his shoulder. "I don't know him so well though; he's very busy."

When we pulled up in front of a handsome, two-story, green-and-white mosque with an adjacent school, there were swarms of white-capped students, mostly teenaged boys, milling around in the shade along the edges of the buildings. Ramli pointed to a small, pastel green house behind the mosque. "That is Tok Guru's house," he said. I paid him and thanked him for driving me.

It was blistering hot outside. The sun was a pulsating, fiery orb that seemed to occupy the whole sky, except for a few crispy-fried clouds. The house was clean but showed its age. The door felt flimsy beneath my knock, which I repeated several times. There was no answer. I stood in the shade of the porch, shuffling my feet as some schoolboys peered around the corner. I spoke with them in halting English for several minutes, finally figuring out that Aziz was at his government office in town and would meet me there. The boys studied Arabic, they said, the better to read the Koran in its original form. They were almost uniformly smiling, curious and

107

friendly. There was no sign of the anti-Americanism that might have been expected, or anti-anything, for that matter. They just seemed like good kids.

I flagged another taxi, while pondering the society of this region. The population was 95 percent Malay-Muslim. Mostly, the people we'd encountered in the two states controlled by the PAS seemed pious, serious about their religion, and family-oriented. The social atmosphere was a bit stuffy and self-righteous, faintly reminiscent of that in the Mormon-dominated Mountain West of the United States: Utah, southern Wyoming, and Idaho. Drinking alcohol was forbidden and almost all the women, with the exception of a few Chinese, wore headscarves. It seemed to be a stable society, if a bit undeveloped compared with Singapore or even the west coast of Peninsular Malaysia, where the country's business and manufacturing was concentrated. The average income in Kelantan was less than one-third what it was in the more developed sections of the country, and many men had to live away from their families to secure jobs.

We arrived at the Kelantan ministerial offices. This was where the seventy-year-old Aziz often held court, his translator whispered as he showed me into a large, high-ceilinged room with curtained windows across the front admitting filmy light that fell on handsome brocaded chairs and a couch, from which several men in traditional Malay dress with white turbans quietly arose and shuffled out of the room. Aziz remained behind. He was not what I expected, which may have been someone perhaps more along the lines of Bashir, the fire-breathing Indonesian jihad cleric. Aziz was a small man, dressed in white with a sash and turban. He had an almost pixie-like quality, a hard twinkle in his eye, and a sparse goat beard, graying and nearly white, typical of the type that was popular in this part of the world.

The translator, an earnest fellow named Anual Bakri Bin Haron who had attended university in England, relayed in Bahasa Malaysia my desire to ask direct questions that meant no disrespect, but that I hoped might help explain Islam and the problems of our times to people such as myself who had little understanding.

This seemed acceptable to Aziz, who smiled and grunted. He said that he had heard Bush had given Saddam twenty-four hours to leave Iraq, and asked me if that was true. I said I thought that it was actually forty-eight hours. He nodded unhappily. It was not a good subject to pursue, and in any case my interests regarding Aziz were closer to home. I asked him how the PAS differed from the ruling United Malays National Organization (UMNO) coalition led by prime minister Mahathir Mohamad.

Aziz crinkled into a grin, then laughed loudly and let loose a torrent of words. "That is very easy. I want to have world peace, and by the look of the world, which is dragged down by wars, drugs, usury, and so many ugly things, it seems that there is something needed. I believe that what is needed is Islam."

That was interesting, but I wondered if Muslims and non-Muslims could live together, or did Muslims require their own Islamist state?

With no hesitation, Aziz replied, "When the Prophet came to the world, he lived beside a mosque, and non-Muslims were there also, and they mixed together. In that spirit, Islam was revealed, so you can see that Islam is there for Muslims and non-Muslims. You do not need an Islamist state."

This was surprising, and somewhat more pleasant than the answer I had anticipated. Certain groups of Muslims, such as the Wahhabi extremists of Saudi Arabia, insisted that they must have an Islamist state. What did he think of that?"

He averted the question. "Please don't refer to the contemporary Islamic societies that live on the earth today," Aziz said. "Look directly at the Prophet and how he lived. We need to stick to the two basic sources, the Koran and the Prophet himself."

That still didn't tell me much about his opinion of those people in this world who did insist upon a pure Islamist state.

He relented, and addressed the question: "I disagree with this. If I were to hold to that sort of principle, Kelantan could not exist as it does."

Was it a good thing to implement Islamic law in Kelantan, where there were people other than Malay-Muslims?

"When we first adapted *hudud* in Kelantan in 1993, we made it clear that it would be up to the people to choose. If you are a non-Muslim and wish to be tried under civil law, it is your choice."

What was his impression of extremist groups such as al Qaeda and Jemaah Islamiyah?

"I only listen to the press," he said. "How much is true, I don't know. Especially in Malaysia, there are always hidden hands controlling things from other places. When the Taliban were in Afghanistan, they controlled the country and were quite popular, but somehow now they are seen as extremists and their image is tarnished. I really don't know."

I felt he knew more about this subject than he was willing to share with me, but pressing him on it seemed unprofitable. Did he favor economic development for Malaysia and for Kelantan?

"Any raw materials provided by Allah are here for the good of humanity, so there is no reason for me not to see development happen, either in Malaysia or in Kelantan."

And the tourist industry along the sea, was that something to be encouraged?

"Why not? Islam urges Muslims to go forth into the world, move around the world and see how beauty is everywhere. You can see this by wandering about. But the problem with the capitalist system is that it looks for profit even at the cost of destruction of various things, and that is why the tourist industry must be controlled. Drinking, sex, sand, sun, all those things they talk about, must be kept under control. We see young backpackers from the West who come here for things that they wouldn't do back home."

It was true. Backpackers swarmed to Southeast Asia in what had become a rite of passage for young Australians, Americans, and Britons and other Europeans, and their behavior was not always in keeping with local traditions. Their search for unspoiled nature and cultures had become both a blessing and a curse to the whole region. I asked Aziz what he thought of the United States and its policies. What did he think America should do in these difficult days since the September 11 terrorist attacks?

That, Aziz said, was a tough question. "The Arab world has been frustrated with America since it recognized Israel in the late 1940s. America has to settle the Palestinian problem, or you will see bombing after bombing. You can see on all the television networks, Israelis killing Palestinians, killing Muslims, and this is the problem that creates men such as Osama bin Laden."

Did he think that if the Palestinian problem were solved, Osama would simply go away?

"If the problem were solved amicably by the Americans, then why should Osama remain? He is a millionaire; he could be living comfortably instead of launching attacks against Americans and hiding out somewhere in the mountains, but he chooses to stay in a cave, and this shows there must be some struggle that Osama is involved in. Why wouldn't he go away if the problem was solved?"

I wasn't certain that the Palestinian terrorist groups such as Hamas and Islamic Jihad that were attacking Israelis wanted or even felt that it would be in their interest to achieve peace. I was certain, however, that Osama, like fifteen of the nineteen suicide hijackers of September 11, was a militant Wahhabi radical who believed in an Islamist state.

"I don't know anything about that, "Aziz said tersely, showing little or no interest in the subject.

There was an element of avoidance or denial in his reluctance to speak in depth about the terrorists, I felt, but again it was his choice. I asked what he thought about the future of Islam in Southeast Asia.

"Let me concentrate on Malaysia," Aziz said, "because what happens here is representative of what happens in Singapore or Indonesia or the Philippines. In Malaysia, you can see the ruling party, UMNO, using its powers to stop the Islamic movement through media, halting political rallies, and acts passed by parliament that oppose Islamic development. Democracy has been used to kill democracy in Malaysia. You can see how it worked in the case of jailing Anwar."

Former deputy prime minister Anwar Ibrahim, a Muslim politician who had been Arabized during his formative years, had once been Mahathir's deputy and anointed successor, but after he bucked the chief on policy during the Asian financial crisis of 1997–98, Anwar was charged with sodomy and with abusing his office, tried, and imprisoned. Homosexuality was viewed as a crime grave enough to merit a prison sentence. Many claimed that Anwar was railroaded on such a charge, while others said that it may well be true. The most interesting fact, perhaps, is that even Nik Aziz believes being gay is a criminal offense, following the view of Shariah.

Were UMNO and Mahathir powerful enough to stop the current Islamist movement in Malaysia?

"PAS is strong here in Kelantan and Terengganu, but the political forces of UMNO always manage to curb our growth. I often think about retiring to live in a *kampung* and take care of my gardening. Then I look at my political responsibility, and at UMNO's policies, and I know that I must answer the call, so I drag my feet along and keep working for our cause."

Was it more important for the rest of the world to learn to live with Islam, or for Islam to learn to live with the world?

Aziz nodded sharply at the translator, suddenly animated, as if he was interested in this question. "Islam has principles, and they are embedded strongly and cannot be challenged. In implementing Islam, there are various techniques, and Islam does not say no to any of them. Take for example, elections. This is a technique of democracy that coincides with Islamic techniques of Shariah, of consultation and the like, so we can accommodate this. Or take for example, tourism. Islam urges the community to travel, to move about, to see places. And you can operate a chalet or a guest house for tourists, but make sure there are no negative things involved, such as drinking, illicit sex, and the like."

Aziz clearly was not possessed by an irrational hatred of outsiders or the ghastly seeking after death that characterized

Qutb, the Wahhabis, and those who had come under their influence. He did show occasional flashes of contempt for those outside the fold encompassed by his religious vision, but that may have been a psychological tool he habitually used for scolding members of his flock to keep them on the straight-and-narrow. I asked if Aziz thought that Islam could operate within a democratic state.

"Islam can definitely operate with democracy," he said confidently, waving a small finger through the air, "but there are certain things that we cannot tolerate. Take for instance, in some European countries, a male can marry with a male, which is legalized by a democratic process. Issues such as this, we cannot accommodate. Islam is based on principles. In times where we can run together with democracy, well, good and fine, but at times when it comes to problems with our principles, then Islam should stay on."

Perhaps that sort of thing, gay marriages, was just a reflection of liberal European culture, I ventured, similar to drinking wine, for example.

"Do not tell me that the Europeans don't know drinking wine is bad for their health."

What was his opinion of Sufism, a type of Islam that was not so concerned with rules, as with direct religious experience? The legalistic Wahhabis despised Sufism, with its mystical leanings, and had long struggled to cut that branch from the tree of Islam within their strongholds on the Arabian Peninsula. Aziz, I knew, was a Sufi.

"Sufism is not so much for rules. The spiritual path is under the guidance of Sufism. If you are stingy or are not thankful for what you have received, then Sufism is the guidance that you may receive under the gurus for this spiritual experience. When we reach a certain level of purity, then we might participate in direct revelation. Through the purification process, through upholding Islamic teachings, we can reach Sufism. I am chief minister now, and I could enjoy great privilege, but I still enjoy living in my small house behind the mosque."

Aziz was a complicated and surprising man whose good qualities and charisma were capable of moving people along like boats on a friendly tide. There was also something troubling about him, but it was beyond the reach of my powers of understanding and articulation, at least for the moment.

Back at the hotel that evening, we drifted off to sleep accompanied by a faraway call to prayers from a mosque. The next day, the war began.

We drove back down to Terengganu, to Tanjong Jara, and that evening I sat with Miwa and Emerson outside at a terrace restaurant on a wooden platform built over a wide brook that eddied softly into a small, tree-lined estuary and out into the sea. Emerson quietly played Pokemon Crystal on his Gameboy. Miwa asked what I was thinking about. The air was warm and perfumed with blossoms, palms rose up toward a bright, silvery moon, and soft gamelan music played by three musicians on a nearby pavilion drifted by dreamily. There was a soft sound of waves in the background and again the pleasant twittering of night birds. The fare was Southeast Asian, fresh fish, chicken, and curries, beautifully prepared and served with efficiency that spoke of Swiss management. It was a memorable pleasure, and still, as reflected moonlight shattered into light and dark fragments on the water's surface, so was my awareness of a lovely evening interpenetrated by thoughts of the war beginning in Iraq. Still, I had the good fortune to be in Malaysia. At least, most of me.

The next day, sitting outside at a tree-shaded bar, Peter told me that most of his guests came from Europe or Japan. "We have the ability to show foreigners what an Islamic country is about and can be, compared to perceptions that many of us have, knowing the Middle East and Northern Africa with their difficulties. Here in Malaysia, we have a certain harmony. It is a safe country." Still, the tourist industry had slowed since September 11 and the Bali terrorist attack, he said, a little sadly.

The controlled approach to tourism that Nik Aziz envisioned, however, one that encouraged resorts but not the creation of another Phuket or Bali swarming with low-budget pleasure seekers, was good. "I can support that strongly," Peter said. "I'm for quality tourism, not quantity. It is quantity tourism that we have in many parts of the world, and we see the damage that it causes to nature and to the environment." The approach of his resort, with more than forty acres and fewer than a hundred units, was more suitable for the region. Nearly all his staff hailed from the surrounding area, and he had used his meticulous Swiss background as a base for training them.

A different sort of tourism was developing in this part of Malaysia, he said, quieter and without the riotous nightlife that the backpacker culture prized, but one that was perhaps preserving more of the natural beauty of the land.

During a snorkeling trip out to Tenggol Island, I asked the dive master, a burly Malaysian with a military bearing, about Nik Aziz. "He has brainwashed too many people," was his blunt opinion. "You know this war with Iraq? They are all against it, against the bombing, but the leaders of the countries ringed around Iraq, they want Saddam out. If you have to live near him, then you don't like him. Around here, they don't even think about that."

And that, perhaps, was what had bothered me about Aziz. He was a good local chieftain. It was when he lifted up his gaze beyond his people and their land, to others, that he lost his focus. Aziz was a Muslim leader of a small Islamic society who drew his principles from the Koran and from his own mystical understandings and applied them within that domain. It could be hoped that he would continue to provide honest leadership to his state and political group, but if the PAS should ever gain power where populations were not heavily Muslim, many of his guiding principles would be quickly called into question. In such an environment, the sound and benign leadership he offered was likely to be perceived as something else, and that would be a shame because he was the real thing, a good man, and that was not a quality to be tossed aside. Aziz was actually more a tribal leader than a political person, and in that situation religion could be seen as a practical component of political organization. By projecting religion-colored rulings into a larger political environment, however, a man such as Aziz could begin to seem arbitrary and even tyrannical. The moral dictums of a religion are not an appropriate substitute for laws of a multicultural state, and Islam, even as interpreted by a Sufi such as Nik Aziz, offered no exception to this.

A few weeks later, the acting president of the PAS, Abdul Hadi Awang, said that if the party came to power throughout Malaysia, it would impose Islamic law and a theocratic state.[5] In a developing country where several religions were represented, for even the largest of them to claim sovereignty over the others was to seek problems. After the eruption of a brief political furor, the PAS withdrew the plan, at least for the time being.

The war in Iraq was fought by an American military that was better, more efficiently integrated, and technologically advanced than a decade earlier in the first Gulf War. Within three weeks the major fighting was over, and the profoundly difficult task remained: that of bringing good government to a regressive country that was essentially a morass of competing interests that had been repressed by a fascist regime for more than three decades.

The establishment of a democratic government in Iraq, which would probably require a number of years if it could be accomplished at all, could ultimately serve not only as a final justification for fighting the war, but also as the first step in an effort to transform the political and social environment of the Middle East, to bring about more responsive governments, and to ease the frustrations of their citizens.

For Americans, the crucial national interest served by this difficult and costly process, should it ultimately succeed, would be the transformation of a troubled region so that it would no longer serve as an ideological breeding ground for global terrorism that could strike in the United States, or for that matter in Southeast Asia or in Europe. The question that will be argued for some time is whether the United States acted successfully in Iraq for the common good of humanity. Many claim that they already know the answer, either pro or con, but they do not, because it will emerge only in the war's political aftermath. In a few years or decades at most, history will provide a factual answer as to whether Iraqis have been enabled to live freer and richer lives, and whether people in surrounding countries are less threatened and somehow influenced to begin transforming their own destinies.

LOOKING FORWARD

Mid-2003—The tourism industry, a significant component of Southeast Asian economies, including Singapore's, was damaged by the Bali bombing, suffered from war in Iraq, and then in early 2003 came a third scourge, that of severe acute respiratory syndrome (SARS), a highly contagious virus that was often deadly. Singapore quickly closed schools, quarantined victims, and scanned travelers for the most common symptom, fever. Still, tourism—which accounted for about a tenth of the economy—plummeted, other industries were hurt as well, and the island twice slashed its forecast for annual economic growth finally to a modest 1 percent. It was not going to be easy, with foreign investment in manufacturing and many of the jobs that had provided decades of economic growth now streaming into lower-cost countries like China.

CHAPTER 6

Singapore's government knew that it was faced with a dire need for a paradigm shift. It must continue to reinvent itself or stagnate. It had to encourage change in the very nature of its people, through its educational system, by retraining, by whatever means possible. There must be a new type of Singaporean, more creative and entrepreneurial, less conservative and not afraid to take a calculated risk when the reward was deemed worthy.

It was not as if Singapore were completely bereft of talented, creative people. Although they had not been particularly encouraged during the long, disciplined drive toward economic development, nevertheless, creative spirits had survived and even flourished during those years when the country was coming to maturity. Let us conclude this story by meeting three of them:

One of the keys to unlocking Singaporean minds will be the elimination of censorship. If there is a single aspect that threatens to hold back Singapore's further development, it could be argued that it is censorship, and yet it is still often viewed as a tool that is useful in keeping people focused on economic advancement. Interestingly enough, my eyes had been drawn some years back to a book club selection because it was "banned in Singapore." The novel was called *The Bondmaid*, and it was written by Catherine Lim. Through a mutual friend, it was arranged for the author to come to dinner, and afterward we sat out on the veranda, surrounded by orchids, ferns, and philodendrons draping from coconut husks, chatting in the warm evening. Lim was an elegant woman in her early sixties with large, sparkling eyes and a kind of vivacious beauty peculiar to female artists.

Her hair was cut stylishly short, and she wore a gold silk scarf set off by a simple black blouse. I asked her about the problems with the novel.

It hadn't been banned, exactly, as it turned out. "I got published internationally because of it. I loved censorship!" she said gleefully. "Actually, in my life as a writer, censorship has had very little impact except in an indirect way with the rejection of *The Bondmaid*, and that wasn't because of the government, but self-imposed by the publishers." The publisher had told her that he was afraid of the book because it was too sexy to clear the government censors. It was a business decision. "I decided to set up my own publishing company in 1995. It was very easy. I published my own book, and it was the best decision I ever made, thanks to censorship." A British literary agent saw the book in Singapore and asked if she could represent the writer. "We signed our contract over chicken rice at the Mandarin Hotel, then she took my book to the Frankfurt Book Fair and that was how I got launched. Isn't that amazing!" Lim laughed in the falsetto way of Chinese women in movies. She was delighted that events had turned in her favor.

Lim said her fiction had not really suffered from the censor, perhaps partly because of her area of interest, which she called the psychodynamics of male–female relationships, set against her Chinese background. "I actually think that this current government is far more tolerant than people believe. The censorship that I am against, however, is that against my political commentaries. I'm sure you've heard about it?"

She had been blasted in the press and on television by various government ministers, referred to as a "fringe writer" who had no right to make comments and made to feel the disapproval of the establishment, although no charges had been filed against her and no official action taken.

Some years back, she had written two political commentaries for the *Straits Times* about what she viewed as the estrangement between Singapore's government and its people. "I live in Singapore and I thought, why don't I draw attention to it. Everybody knows about it. There is this emotional estrangement from the government, or dissonance, whereby Singaporeans say, 'We appreciate your hard work and effectiveness but we don't like you because you talk down to us and lecture us.' They were arrogant, you know? Now, my point was that in the Lee Kuan Yew dispensation this was probably the thing to do. The population was naive; all they wanted was sanitation and a clean house, and Lee Kuan Yew could do this. Clean up the street and it's what they wanted."

He had certainly done that.

"He did beautifully. You know, you've got to give credit, this man has done a great deal for Singapore. But he was also astute enough to realize that there was a new generation, more educated, more exposed, more articulate, and his style might not go down so well with them. He put Goh Chok Tong into power, although they say he's still the man behind the scenes. Anyway, after my first article, I wrote another, called 'One Government, Two Styles,' and they jumped. I said they were sending out confusing signals, and that Singaporeans were not sure what was happening. I see it now. Many Singaporeans even today don't put out the flag for National Day because they say they don't want to be seen as sycophantic toward the People's Action Party, but the flag is the national flag of Singapore! So there's a great deal of confusion with regard to this thing called loyalty." Singaporeans' loyalty, in her view, was to the good life that had been created by the People's Action Party, not toward the party itself. Singaporeans were creatures of self-interest, she said, combining gesture and expression with her words to convey her shifting states of mind. Lim had a dramatic flair that must have flowed easily onto the page when she wrote.

But wasn't self-interest an important factor, I asked. Didn't it drive people to work hard, to do a number of good things?

"It's not a bad thing," Lim said. "Except that you shouldn't try to gloss over your motives with all sorts of moral reasons for acting as you do. But my main point is that no matter how efficient the government is, in the event of an external crisis, you still need a robust, politically savvy civil society, which we don't have. We are among the most politically naive people in the world."

Why was that?

"Because of Lee Kuan Yew. Lots of things are traceable to him, both good and bad. He thinks that the relationship between the people and the government should be this: You vote us in, which means you trust us, so leave us to do our job; don't stand around and criticize us. All he wants is minimal political engagement every five years; you vote responsibly, and that's it. Then you go make money, you buy your second home, you raise your children, but you leave us to do our job and if we fail, if we are corrupt, you vote us out of power. This is Lee Kuan Yew. It is actually very good, very noble, and far better than what we have seen around Southeast Asia." It was the Singapore tradition. The government had never encouraged a civil society. It was a preemptive government, which was good for solving problems like a water crisis or joblessness, but you could not treat people like that forever.

Now they were beginning to see that, Lim said. They were opening up. "So, political openness, bit by bit. They do a dance, they give you four steps; if you're misbehaving, they pull you back two steps. Of course, there will be a net increase in the end. But it is too little and too slow."

People had an obligation to say something, didn't they?

"Yes, but a political culture takes time, it is organic, and to be authentic it has to grow. And we don't have so much time, so it is a conundrum, a problem, like creativity. This is something that is not of the norm. Artists are like madmen; they are completely free and have their own way, but Singapore cannot take that, so given its tradition of always being in control, creativity is managed here, political openness is managed, and I think that's going to be our problem." Singapore's government should relax now and allow a complete political education, she said. They could afford some dissonance. They should allow Singaporeans to grow, or they would forever be like delicate plants raised in hothouse nurseries.

There have been signs in recent years that the government, under Prime Minister Goh Chok Tong, is doing that, is trying to loosen up, with perhaps spotty results. There was a public relations campaign, for example, to demonstrate that Singapore is indeed a "funky town" that has its own wild side to walk on. And it does have a vibrant dining out and nightclubbing scene, although "funky" might be going too far. A local comedian and female impersonator, Kumar, has become a star, appearing in Singapore television dramas and theaters. There was also a campaign to develop "little bohemias," which were deemed as necessary for the growth of anything resembling Silicon Valley, a phenomenon that is greatly desired. An expatriate enclave called Holland Village was cited as an example. And while "Holland V" may well be popular among expats, you will find there are many more investment bankers than "bohemians," artists, poets, or musicians. The government went on, however, to announce that it would allow dancing on bartops, and even that its policy had been quietly changed to allow homosexuals to hold government jobs, which was not a small step in Singaporean society.

One surprising occurrence was the appearance for two nights of the Rolling Stones, a band whose reputation preceded them so far that while they were to be allowed to play Beijing after the Singapore gigs, they were issued a list of their songs deemed unsuitable for the pure ears of their fans in China, which included "Brown Sugar" and other rockers with suggestively sexual or rebellious lyrics. Of course, they opened the Singapore concerts with that song, the venerable Keith Richards sliding into a spotlight in a cobalt-blue coat with tails, cranking out the power chords with a sheepish grin. Later, before the introduction of "Honky Tonk Women," giant cheerleader dolls inflated on either side of the stage with flagpoles stuck in their crotches, one with a Rolling Stones banner baring its lewd tongue, and the other with a Singapore flag proudly unfurled. This was more like it. I was told that the next night, however, the flags were missing from the act. And the Beijing gig never came off, with or without "Brown Sugar," because the SARS epidemic flared up and the Stones decided, quite wisely at the time, that it was better for all concerned to cancel.

The effort to change the tone of Singapore faintly echoed one by Japan's government a decade earlier, when they too realized that their economy had achieved most of the growth possible through its developmental catch-up strategy, and that they had to devise new products on their own; they had to become "creative" if they were to continue their economic expansion. Japan's Ministry of Education proposed that it might therefore begin teaching creativity in schools, along with subjects like mathematics and language. Then the problems began. First, no one in the ministry seemed quite sure what it meant to be "creative," and second, they did manage to ascertain that it would mean allowing a degree of social freedoms that would result in the next generation of students thinking for themselves more than the government was comfortable with. The idea was allowed to die a quiet death, along with the country's rapid economic growth. The fact was, Japan had enough money not to worry about growth rates for some time to come. It was the world's biggest creditor nation. Not so, Singapore. The city-state was also a great developmental success story, but it was small, without a hinterland and therefore fragile, with a $90 billion economy compared to Japan's $3 trillion. Singapore would have to find its own way forward in this unexplored territory, without a Japanese model to show the way.

Kirpal Singh is a Sikh, follower of a monotheistic religion formed about five hundred years ago in India. Sikh gurus have criticized both Hinduism and Islam for stressing outer forms rather than aiming for spiritual awakening. Singh does not cut his hair and wears a beard as well as the traditional turban of his sect, although his family has been Singaporean for generations. He is a noted Asian poet and was a longtime English professor at the National University of Singapore before joining Singapore Management University, which has been charged with helping train a new generation of

Singaporean entrepreneurs and managers. This generation must be prepared to cope with the emerging realities of the nation's future, including enhanced freedoms and the heavier burdens of individual responsibility that accompany them. Singh, who teaches creativity, finds himself with a considerable job before him: spearheading a shift in the island's school system, which has for decades been geared to turning out the most efficient factory workers possible, and which now must begin to educate a wider range of students that will include spirited risk-takers who it is hoped will be able to help lead the economy going ahead.

What was the relationship, I asked Singh, between censorship and creativity, the protean quality that everyone agreed must be a part of Singapore's future if the economy was to find new ways to grow?

One of the reasons creativity had been stifled in Singapore, he said, was that there had been all manners of censorship. "Let's begin with censorship by the state. Because Lee Kuan Yew was pretty sure about what he wanted, he was convinced that to build a road from where we were thirty years ago to where we are now, the way would be blocked and hampered if he allowed a free play of ideas. Because of that, he exerted control. He was blunt about it. He said, look, we have no time for writers, dreamers sitting under coconut trees with ideas, sociologists, political scientists, all these kinds of people, because we must finish building one road, and the free play of ideas would very likely divert us from that, so we would end up with many roads instead, none of which would be complete."

Lee had been in a hurry to arrive at his destination, which was the economic development of Singapore, and he clamped down on a lot of things, including creativity in the arts and culture. "I'm not saying Lee Kuan Yew was wrong, In fact there is much virtue in what he did, because for a society to appreciate the very creativity that might exist within it, it does need the hospitals, the schools, the roads, the houses, everything. When there's no bread, it is difficult to appreciate the things beyond bread. It's like Christ, you break bread and make sure everybody's well fed, then you deliver your sermon, and people can talk about the sermon, their interpretations and so forth. . . . That's my analogy." Singh smiled. His beard was touched with gray that hinted at his years. He liked to color-coordinate blue or green silk shirts with the yards of material that he wound each day into his turban. He had recently finished writing a book about creativity, called *Thinking Hats and Coloured Turbans: Creativity Across Cultures*, which would be a textbook for Singaporean students.

Censorship and diminished creativity in Singapore had been necessary, and sometimes from the creative person's point of view, unfortunate, but it had helped the nation arrive at a higher developmental state without undue hindrance. People had been fed, babies had been born and were able to flourish and grow, and through the Housing Development Board program modern homes had been made available for almost everybody.

"In the past three years the government has come around to saying, hey, we need creative people, we want creativity to blossom. Unfortunately, the machinery that has been introduced to get us where we are today is so rigid that the very creativity the government wants is often suppressed by its own infrastructure that was needed to get us from Third World to First World."

Why couldn't things continue to evolve as they were? What was the actual importance of bringing a sort of abstract quality such as creativity to Singapore?

Creativity was breaking barriers, challenging norms, going beyond the accepted, he said. To achieve even a small measure, there must be a lot of undoing. Many of the institutional structures had to be dismantled. "Like Japan's educational system, Singapore has facilitated manufacturing in an efficiency-driven economic model. This is not appropriate, however, for a knowledge-driven economy, because it is difficult to manage knowledge with rigid controls in place."

Was Singapore really transforming itself from one kind of economy to another?

It was, but it was arriving at a knowledge-based economy that emphasized financial services and so forth a little too quickly for some people, and there were still old-line bureaucrats occupying many seats of power with a few years left before retirement. They didn't want to let go, even though some of the younger cabinet ministers desired exactly that. "So I see a big tussle here," Singh said, "between a more creative approach, on the one hand, and these bureaucrats who have been sitting on the infrastructure of administration. I think the general political will of Singapore favors moving ahead, and the creative people are prepared to offer what they have, but in the middle they are blocked by this bureaucracy and red tape, what Dickens would have called the Circumlocution Office. It is always there." The nation itself had to set an example to encourage creativity. "You cannot say be creative, then punish the guy who in being creative has questioned a few of your values!" He laughed uproariously. I'd gotten to know Singh and had noticed that he was a master at influencing the emotional environment, at modulating the tone of a friendly, jovial, or occasionally even a raucous gathering. He was a man who brought something, some kind of special energy, to the party.

I wondered, though, how could a nation, even a small city-state like Singapore that is certainly easier to manipulate than, say, Japan with its much larger size and cultural rigidities, hope to transform the nature of its people to enhance their creative abilities?

There were two ways, he thought, and both involved education. One was education through the normal channels, nurseries, kindergartens, where you may simply teach the ABCs, or approach it more in a *Sesame Street* manner and say, well, let's examine the letter B first, before we go on. This expanded the potential to explore and learn, as opposed to simply learning the correct order. "I also think that education through contact is important. This is where you would not censor the information flow from other countries, where you allow the global movements that involve ways of looking at the world to come in unfiltered. I think Singapore is trying to get there. There is a lot of media that comes into Singapore uncensored; in fact, there's not much that can be done about it these days, and there are a lot of media reports that are dispatched from Singapore in the same way." Those were two major ways, but there was also a third, and that was allowing creative people to become national icons, because the icons of Singapore were mostly political or business leaders. "Of course you can also be creative as a politician, and I think Lee Kuan Yew has been supremely creative as a political entity. But there are others."

I thought of Kumar, and also of Jack Neo, a local filmmaker who had been mentioned in some recent speeches by Prime Minister Goh. There were things happening, still small, but taken together they might eventually come to be seen as a beginning. How did Singh think that Singapore would progress in this direction, not what would he like to see happen, but what did he think would actually happen?

"In the next five to ten years there will probably be a bit more chaos as we become a more creative nation. Some of the systems that are now intact may find themselves challenged and perhaps even pushed past their limits. I think it is happening because the political will is there, and it is the only way Singapore is going to survive." Singh said he didn't think the city-state could continue to produce a uniform, factory-oriented, mass-manufacturing kind of workforce. As Singapore approached the higher reaches of a technologically driven economy, he reckoned that some people would lose their jobs, there would be a lot of soul searching, and obsolete organizations would be dismantled, followed by increased devolution of power and more decentralized control. Smaller organizations would come into being, within which creativity would be encouraged. Then if things went wrong in the early stages, it could be contained and not be so widespread as to undermine the entire national fabric.

Were Singaporeans up to managing a democratic state at the present time?

"Yes and no. Some Singaporeans are well educated and politically sensitive, and they are ready for the kind of democracy that America or the United Kingdom would entertain. But my feeling is that 60 percent of Singaporeans are not ready for that. We are still not there." One of the things bothering the leadership was how to introduce an American-style democracy without making people terribly insecure—the kind of insecurity associated with religious freedom, racial, ethnic, and sectarian interests. "It's very complex, but if we continue in the direction we are proceeding in now, slowly and firmly, within twenty years we will arrive in a state where we will be as ready as any nation for democracy."

Others think that Singapore's educated citizens may be ready even sooner. Writer Fareed Zakaria says it is inevitable within fifteen years. He points out that Singapore is the only country—with the exception of oil states that depend on the exports of that single commodity for their wealth—with a per capita GDP of more than $10,000 that is not yet democratic. "Singapore already has very strong strands of constitutional liberalism. It has a vigorous free economy, and rights of property, belief, travel, etc., are staunchly protected. The country is open to the world."[1]

As you pass time in the city, you cannot help but awaken to a sense that Singaporeans are looking ahead with both hope and dread to the post–Lee Kuan Yew period that approaches, because the country's patriarch cannot live forever. When Lee departs, however, he will leave behind the legacy of a foundation. When you look closely at Singapore over several years, it becomes clear that its basic plan, the skyline, the waterfront, seaport, airport, green spaces, condominiums, shophouses, colonial buildings, business district, and palm-fringed bungalows, all of it, well-planned, smoothly functioning, efficient, and prosperous, is here because Lee Kuan Yew has willed it. Singapore is in many ways a reflection of Lee's mind, in the sense that Indonesia's poverty and corruption echo decades of Suharto, or that the modern Philippines were formed by the unleashed greed of Ferdinand Marcos and his cronies. Singapore, with its beauty, its solid economy, and its constant striving, and indeed, its flaws as well, is in that sense the creation of Lee Kuan Yew's character. He had help, much of it able, but his judgment was always final, the responsibility always his. In Lee's achievement there must be enormous satisfaction, but that must entwine with anxiety as the small state sails into a future in which he will no longer be around to navigate. As Lee said, there is no predicting what powerful outside forces will act on Singapore or what government will take shape. Lee's son, Lee Hsien Loong, was named by Prime Minister Goh as his eventual successor. The elder Lee has also appointed committees of able people to study both the problems and the potential for Singapore as it moves into its next phase. He has done all that he can.

Tan Chong Kee met me at a Starbuck's coffee shop in Singapore's heartland. A Stanford Ph.D., he had launched a dotcom company that went belly-up in the bust, and was sitting on the board of a multiethnic theater group as he considered his options for a new business foray. Although he was a member of the Remaking Singapore Committee, which was charged with envisioning and evaluating proposals for continuing the transformation of the island-state, Tan emphasized that he spoke in a personal capacity. He had no shortage of ideas, which would seem to indicate that Singapore will be able to choose from an array of options. How important, I asked, was education in changing the way Singapore did business?

Singapore's success had come about because it emphasized free trade and a free market, Tan said. It had done that by making clear laws about property ownership and transactions and upholding them in court. The problem was that this model had been constructed and fine-tuned for an industrial age when manufacturing power was the main source of wealth. Much of the manufacturing was now shifting to lower-wage countries, especially to China. "The countries that are more developed are trying to move up the value chain and make their money through design, through innovation, through higher technology. So, the old system that we have is somewhat outmoded. Our educational system creates good workers for manufacturing. If we want to transform ourselves into a different kind of economy, with people who innovate, who take risks and make business deals, who do more than assembling parts, it will require a very different kind of workforce and very different kind of citizen."

The primary schools were terrific, I said, but Singapore's secondary schools may eventually let them down if they were not reconfigured.

"Yes, that's why there is reform going on now, trying to change them." The system still worked on the old paradigm of conformity, don't ask any questions, do as you're told. What Singapore needed was not just educational reform, but a basic rethink of the whole country. How could you move from a paradigm of speed, conformity, and the assembly line to one that was a bit chaotic, with people taking risks and assuming the responsibility for them? Almost everything needed to be reformed. "Take mass media," Tan said. "The *Straits Times* was a newspaper for the purpose of nation building. They don't criticize state policy, because the media is to be used to mobilize the nation in whatever direction the state decides to be good."

The developmental state media was much like that in Japan, I thought, where I'd worked for two newspaper companies.

Yes, and Singapore had to do something about that. It could

not have a controlled media on the one hand and yet try to emphasize a more creative citizenry on the other. So how could they bring about a different sort of media? "We currently have a duopoly, with two companies that take direct cues from the state. The best way to get out of this, I think, is complete liberation of the media. Let anyone compete in a free market that is much like the one for goods. Let there be free competition among media, ideas, and knowledge, so the fittest will emerge and in the process we will eventually have companies that will be consistent with our aim of an upgraded media. Similarly, we need an overhaul of our electoral politics. Previously, the thinking was that we needed a very strong state with control of parliament so that decisions could be made very quickly and everyone would fall in line and get it done."

The guidance had come from the very top of the pyramid, and that system had worked well for almost four decades, hadn't it?

"It worked extremely well," Tan said. "Long debates were not needed, and things happened. We had America and Japan showing us the way, how to manufacture, giving us a clear indication of what needed to be done. The answers were out there for all to see, so there was little need for debate; it was more a question of resolve, of pulling your socks up and doing it. But now, we are in uncharted territory. Everyone is looking for the model, and no one knows what the model is."

There was no model to emulate, now that Asian frontrunner Japan had ceased to move ahead. It seemed that each developmental country—once it had achieved economic maturity—must make it own choices about what it wished to be, and then do its best to realize them.

"Since there are no longer any clear answers, if you still wish to make quick decisions, chances are increased that the wrong ones may be made. We need to have a lot of debate, so that whatever decision we make is more likely to be the right one. And because we will have a lot of debate, whatever wrong decisions we make will be reviewed and challenged and re-formulated. The kind of system we have now, unfortunately, is not the best for this kind of process." Tan displayed an earnestness of a sort that was sometimes seen among Northern Californian idealists, a quality that he may have been exposed to or developed during his studies in Palo Alto. There was not a trace of irony or cynicism emanating from him.

Japan, upon reaching maturity and slowing growth rates, had cautiously tried to make some changes, I said, but had been constrained by its culture and threatened political elites. As a multiethnic state, Singapore did not carry such a heavy cultural burden. It might have more potential for transformation.

"But Singapore is bound by its institutions," Tan said.

Perhaps. Still, institutions weren't as difficult to overcome as countless generations of ingrained cultural and political behavior, which was what had bound Japan so tightly.

"So far, there are still not many signs that we are changing, although we are trying to urge some very fundamental changes."

What actual, pragmatic directions would he advocate his country taking?

"We are more interested in changing the process by which decisions are arrived at, in putting together guidelines for debate and for cultural groups to interact and achieve more social cohesion."

How would Tan encourage the Malay-Muslim portion of the Singaporean community, to keep it from splitting off socially and moving with the current global Islamic movement, given that some people may try to take it in that direction?

State policy had prohibited public discussion of race or religion, so there had been little interaction between races and religions, except in schools. "We haven't tried to understand each other's faith and values," Tan said, "and that had been fine when there were no problems. The differences are kind of hidden. I think that to have a really stable society it is crucial to have more understanding of the cultures that live side by side. We shouldn't immediately suspect each other of terrorism or something the moment something happens. As you can see, the Chinese are freaked out at the present time about the Muslims. In order not to have this sort of reaction, it requires more understanding and friendship, so that we have enough Malay friends to know what they are really like."

The current situation had thrown into defined relief the problem of loyalty to a religion conflicting with that to the state, Tan said, and it was unfortunate that Muslims sometimes felt they had to choose between the two. Was there a way to manage things so that people of different religions didn't feel that they must choose? More civil society–initiated dialogues between communities could help reduce misunderstanding and suspicions. A framework was needed so that more interaction occurred in a productive way. This would not mean that people wouldn't get angry or feel slighted. Singapore shouldn't try to prevent that. "What we want to prevent are riots, violence, terrorism, and those sorts of things. If we have a Muslim community in Singapore that feels isolated, that feels poorly integrated and somehow threatened by state policies, the pull from outside will be strong. If they feel they have a state that understands their needs, then the pull from outside will be less relevant. So how do we put in place a system that allows the Malay-Muslims to acquire a bit more of the ethos of capitalism, but does not threaten them, and that is peaceful and does not lead to the al Qaeda–style of terrorism we see today?"

Tan's reply seemed to have reformulated my question. It was a difficult question. Would the Singapore government agree with the sweeping and fundamental sort of changes that Tan was advocating?

"No, we probably will not get them all this time around," he said, regretfully.

It is an ideal that Tan is in search of, or a path toward one that leads to enhanced freedom, and, as such, a direction that cannot be faulted, although two dangers can be identified: the constant difficulty of maintaining a healthy economy and therefore the creation of jobs and incomes needed by Singaporeans to raise and continue to educate their families, and that of a splintering off of the Malay-Muslim community into a social group that could increasingly view the Chinese and Indians as outsiders, to be mistrusted and avoided. Tan and the government seemed to agree that the old solutions may not be sufficient, and the way ahead presented a tangled complex of economic, social, and religious issues that must be approached with good will and resolved to serve the needs of all Singaporeans.

An e-mail arrived from Zulfikar, who was in Australia, where he said he had become a research fellow at Monash Asia Institute and was also working with colleagues to bring democracy to Singapore, a country to which he intended to return in the future. The thought occurred that if his timing was appropriate, Zulfikar could very well make a successful return to a democratizing Singapore and offer a contribution.

Kirpal Singh and Fareed Zakaria are probably right about Singapore: It does seem destined to become a liberal democracy as its prosperous middle class gains in influence and power. Over the past six years, it has taken a battering—the Asian financial crisis of 1997–98, the Jemaah Islamiyah roundups, the Bali bombing, wars in Afghanistan and Iraq, and finally the SARS epidemic—and still its economy was expanding, albeit slowly. Entering the next phase of its development will be difficult, for there is no well-trodden path to follow. There will be failures along the way, but Singapore is a survivor. Its people will work hard, the city-state will continue to evolve politically and it will participate meaningfully in the economic systems of global capitalism.

Still, there are pitfalls along the way. History says that city-states are fragile; many have risen, only to be absorbed into larger political entities. Athens and Venice were once commercially powerful city-states. For Singapore to remain cohesive and affluent, it must remain open and pluralistic, while also developing a strong sense of national identity.[2] It is important that the visionary power of Singapore's leaders bonds its citizens as they develop a civil society for the drive toward a democratic government that will operate with the efficiency needed to keep it at the cutting edge of Asian development. Open debate of issues would be healthy. Fragmentation and bitter partisanship would create more dissonance than it could easily bear. Minister for Muslim affairs Yaacob Ibrahim told participants in an Islamic awareness seminar they must "always remember that we are Singaporeans first. Our historical and cultural threads point toward today's reality, that whether we are Malays, Chinese, Indians, Eurasians, or any other race, our lives as Singaporeans are interwoven into a common tapestry, a common destiny." For a mere 3 million citizens to produce a powerhouse economy and keep it growing, there must be a clear awareness of that common destiny. It should be tended like a prize garden.

The regional tourism industry, which was so badly damaged, will come back eventually, although millions of jobs and billions of dollars have been lost. But where else in the world can one find such white-sand beaches, clear waters, and azure skies? The natural resources will await the return of the tourists, from Bali to the beautiful northeast countryside of Peninsular Malaysia, where Nik Aziz and his Parti Islam SeMalaysia hold sway.

Indonesia, which had lingered in denial that it had any problems with terrorism, finally took the threat seriously and put the cleric Bashir on trial for treason, despite an overtly public presence of his following of militant jihadis. He continued to deny any knowledge of Jemaah Islamiyah, although detained members testified via videoconference from Singapore and Malaysia that he was indeed their guru and leader.

In Bali, the "smiling bomber" Amrozi and several cohorts, including two of his brothers, went on trial for the murder of more than two hundred people. Amrozi was unrepentant on the stand, where he said that the victims' deaths served them right. One of his main justifications for murder was his contention that Westerners had introduced videos and "colonized late-night television,"[3] which was destroying the lives of Indonesians.

In a move that may have been a calculated warning of what to expect if Amrozi were to be convicted, just days before the verdict in early August, a Jemaah Islamiyah suicide bomber drove a vehicle to the glassed-in front of the JW Marriott hotel in Jakarta, where it exploded, killing 12 people and wounding about 150. Al Qaeda later claimed a share of the responsibility for the blast in a statement released to Arab media. Police were able to identify the bomber after recovering his head from the hotel's fifth floor. His name was Asmar Latinsani, he was in his late twenties, and he "had attended a hard-line Islamic school headed by Abu Bakar Bashir."[4] The school produced about 1,800 graduates each year.

Nevertheless, two days later, Amrozi was found guilty of supplying bomb materials and the minivan used in the Bali blast, and sentenced to death by firing squad. Upon hearing his sentence, the terrorist shouted, "God is great!" as instructed by al Qaeda manuals. He pumped his fist like a winning athlete, turned and gave a smiling thumbs-up to his legal defense team. Amrozi was not an ideologically motivated intellectual. He was a simple man, little more than a racist who hated white people and Western videos. His prejudices had been utilized, his fantasies transformed into fear, aggression, and violence. He became another of Bashir's martyrs.

A week later, Jemaah Islamiyah operational commander Hambali was caught in Thailand. He had been living quietly in a tourist town, where he was busily plotting to bomb a summit of the twenty-one member heads of state from the Asia-Pacific Economic Cooperation (APEC) forum scheduled for Bangkok in October.

Bashir, in a final statement before the court, tried to avoid prison by warning a panel of judges that if he were found guilty, they would face the wrath of God and be consigned to hell.[5] The judges apparently did not believe that Bashir had as much cosmic influence as the threat implied. Still, they went easy on the sixty-five-year-old cleric in early September, when they sentenced him to four years in jail for his involvement in a violent plot to overthrow the government, but claimed there was not enough evidence to prove he was the leader of Jemaah Islamiyah. Prosecutors, who had demanded a fifteen-year sentence, said they would appeal the decision in an effort to keep Bashir behind bars for a longer stretch.

Progress was made, although many terrorist cells remained intact and victory seemed distant. Violent Islamists around the world were pursued, jailed, or killed, but others continued to launch attacks and target Westerners. Terrorism will not go away soon, because the pathological intolerance of Islamists is a disease, a spiritual epidemic that managed to take hold in vulnerable points around the globe before anyone realized its virulence and moved to contain its spread.

An international poll taken by the Pew Research Center and released after the Iraq war showed that anti-Americanism had soared in Muslim countries, and that Osama bin Laden was trusted by many as a leader who would "do the right thing."[6] A Muslim friend told me that when America went to war against Afghanistan and Iraq, although President Bush took pains to say it was not Islam but terrorism that was the enemy, he could not help but feel that in some way Islam was under attack. "My identity is bound up with Islam," said my friend. He sighed and supposed that such strong psychological identities were probably why peoples felt prejudice and hatred toward one another. Group identities are basic to our natures, and it is only in recent decades that we have begun trying to create pluralistic communities characterized by tolerance and equal rights. Can we be flexible enough to take part in many groups, to glide in and out of them with grace and detachment? Can we rouse the strength to stand alone when appropriate? That will be a long road that we must each walk down.

Terrorism is engaged on many fronts, and while we have not seen a nuclear explosion from a container ship obliterating New York, or a sarin gas attack in London's underground, such horrors are all too possible. The cold war is long over. We have entered an age of terror, although it is a conflict the terrorists are bound to lose. They cannot win, largely because humanity will ultimately judge that they are morally wrong, and more directly because of Western military and intelligence efforts against them, but they will probably kill many, many innocent people in their jihad, as that has become their official, and quite pointless, aim.

Still, contrary to urban legends in the Muslim Street, as the ranks of terrorists are decimated, that is not likely to spawn more bombers, but fewer. In May 2003, al Qaeda launched a suicide attack on a compound in Riyadh, Saudi Arabia, killing foreigners as well as Saudi Muslims, and that country finally began to remove its most radical clerics from their mosques. The nation's de facto ruler, Crown Prince Abdullah, warned ordinary Saudis not to back the terrorists. "In the decisive battle between powers of good and evil, there is no room for neutrality or hesitancy. He who protects or sympathizes with a terrorist is himself a terrorist."[7] It will take time to turn things around because the Islamists have had several decades to take root, but any movement that leads only to chaos and death, even with a bogus promise of paradise, must finish a loser. Most people try to find their brief moments of paradise here on earth, and while those moments never last long, they are what we can claim if we work for them, raise our families well, and try to realize whatever potential we have. Our right to pursue this earthly happiness is worth fighting for, and most Americans realize that. They also know that a system that creates fanatics whose most fervent desire is to kill us must be transformed or put out of business.

There can be no doubt that many conservative Muslims perceive the Western world, with its racy movies and videos, bars and nightclubs, rock and rap music, its liberated women, philandering politicians, and gay marriages as threatening to their way of life. Still, the world will not shift into reverse for them, progressive culture will not turn back despite the worst that terrorists can do. The president of Iran, Mohammad Khatami, said, "We must concede that the incompatibility of modern civilization with our tradition-bound civilization is one of the most important causes of the crisis in our society."[8] He rhetorically asked whether his society should remain tied to its tradition or blend fully into Western civilization. Then he allowed for a third way—accepting modern civilization as an unfinished creation, and entering into a dialogue with it that would ultimately strengthen Muslim culture into a world-dominating position. Fair enough to try, but one wonders if this is not just more delusion. Even young Iranians have wearied of the heavy-handed rule of the *mullahs*.

A question that naturally arises for Westerners is what does Islam have to offer the world?

When Japan rebuilt after World War II, it brought manufacturing techniques and a method of developing states to modernity within decades that could be emulated, as Singapore has demonstrated. Germany created a federal democracy and showed that it had the vision to help unify Europe and avoid, it is hoped, the sort of catastrophic wars it initiated in the past century. Certainly, progressive civilization is by its nature unfinished and imperfect, but shouldn't leaders of Islamic cultures and states, rather than seeking to dominate, be asking what they can offer the world to influence and benefit the progress of humanity?

Islamic culture is not tied to one specific nation, nor is it particularly uniform in its religious interpretations. This rules out certain responses, but may allow for others. Because the global Islamic community is widespread and fragmented, a clearly necessary skill is that of living peacefully with neighboring religions and ethnic groups. "When the Prophet came to the world, he lived beside a mosque, and non-Muslims were there also, and they mixed together. In that spirit, Islam was revealed," Nik Aziz had told me. By developing such abilities to an advanced level as a living example, Islam could offer a profound gift to the world that is sorely needed at a time when weapons have been created that can destroy whole cities in blinding flashes of fire. Such a gift would be of inestimable value to humanity. It almost seems too much to hope for. But only hope, harnessed with desire and hard work, can lead to better things. So let us hope, and continue to work.

Parallel to that, the ability to integrate all of its races and religions into a coherent, smoothly functioning whole remains one of the keys to Singapore's economic and political future. Its progress may come to be measured by how successfully it manages that task.

CHAPTER 6

The practical efforts of Singapore to bring Muslims, like everyone else, into its economic, cultural, and intellectual life, to understand that they are part of us, and hope that they return this favor and see us also as "different but worthy of respect," may offer a bellwether. If a healthy pluralistic society can be created and maintained in Singapore, there is no reason why it cannot be so elsewhere, or even everywhere.

NOTES

Notes to Chapter 1

1. Richard Winstedt, *The Malays: A Cultural History* (London: Routledge & Kegan Paul, 1947), 137–38.

2. Christopher Lane, ed., *The Psychoanalysis of Race* (New York: Columbia University Press, 1998), 13, quoting Sigmund Freud, *Group Psychology and the Analysis of the Ego*, vol. 18 of *The Standard Edition of the Complete Psychological Works of Sigmund Freud*, ed. and trans. James Strachey (London: Hogarth, 1953–74), 65–144.

3. Winstedt, *The Malays*, 135.

4. Pang Eng Fong, "The Economic Status of Malay Muslims in Singapore," *Journal Institute of Muslim Minority Affairs* 111, no. 2 (Winter 1981): 150.

5. Winstedt, *The Malays*, 137.

6. Ibid., 138.

7. Lily Zubaidah Rahim, *The Singapore Dilemma: The Political and Educational Marginality of the Malay Community* (Kuala Lumpur: Oxford University Press, 2001), 61.

8. Cherian George, *Singapore: The Air-Conditioned Nation* (Singapore: Landmark Books, 2000), 67.

9. Ibid., 47

10. Kishore Mahbubani, *Can Asians Think?* (Singapore: Times Books International, 1998), 185–86.

11. Fareed Zakaria, "The Politics of Rage: Why Do They Hate Us?" *Newsweek*, October 15, 2001; available at www.fareedzakaria.com/articles/newsweek/101501_why.html.

Notes to Chapter 2

1. Samuel P. Huntingon, *The Clash of Civilizations and the Remaking of World Order* (New York and London: Touchstone Books, 1996), 252.

2. Karen Armstrong, *The Battle for God* (New York: Random House, 2000), 64.

3. Michael Scott Doran, "Somebody Else's Civil War," *Foreign Afairs* 82, no. 1 (January–February 2002): 22.

4. "Live with Others in Peace: Mufti," *Straits Times*, October 2, 2001, 1.

5. Ibid.

6. "Terrorists Tried to Recruit S'poreans," *Straits Times*, October 15, 2001, 1.

7. "SM: We Have to Remake Singapore," *Straits Times*, October 16, 2001, 1.

8. Lee Kuan Yew, *From Third World to First* (Singapore: Straits Times Press, 2000), 39.

9. V.S. Naipaul, *Among the Believers* (New York: Random House, 1981), 355.

10. John L. Esposito, *Unholy War: Terror in the Name of Islam* (New York: Oxford University Press, 2002), 7.

11. Stephen Schwartz, *The Two Faces of Islam: The House of Sa'ud from Tradition to Terror* (New York: Doubleday, 2002), xiii–xiv.

12. Esposito, *Unholy War*, 49.

13. Bernard Lewis, *What Went Wrong? Western Impact and Middle Eastern Response* (New York: Oxford University Press, 2002), 159.

14. Schwartz, *The Two Faces of Islam*,180.

Notes to Chapter 3

1. "At Religious Boarding School in Java, bin Laden Is a Hero," *International Herald Tribune*, February 4, 2002, 2.

2. "Malay/Muslim Leaders Here Back Gov't Crackdown," *Straits Times*, January 6, 2002, 1.

3. "Terror, Lies and Videotape," *Today*, January 12, 2002, 1.

4. Media statement by Yatiman Yusof in response to Fateha CEO's claims, January 19, 2002.

5. "PM Firm on Tudung Issue," *Sunday Times*, February 3, 2002, 1.

6. "Mufti Puts School First," *Straits Times*, February 6, 2002, 1.

7. "Security, Harmony the Main Worry Now," *Straits Times*, February 11, 2002, 1.

8. Arthur J. Deikman, *The Wrong Way Home: Uncovering the Patterns of Cult Behavior in American Society* (Boston: Beacon Press, 1990), 89.

9. Ibid., 106.

10. "PAS Men Try to Stop Police Concert," *Straits Times*, September 10, 2002, A7.

11. "What's His Game?" *Today*, July 8, 2002, 1.

12. Ibid.

13. "Ex-Fateha Leader Flees to Melbourne," *Straits Times*, July 25, 2002, 4.

Notes to Chapter 4

1. Michael Skube, "If Liberalism's Such a Dead Horse, Why Beat It?" *Washington Post*, April 20, 2003; available at www.washingtonpost.com.

2. Paul Berman, *Terror and Liberalism* (New York: Norton, 2003), 87.

3. "The Jemaah Islamiyah Arrests and the Threat of Terrorism," Singapore Government White Paper, 2003, 17.

4. Hechmi Dhaoui, "From Wahhabism to Talibanism," in *A Global Nightmare: Jungian Reflections on September 11*, ed. Luigi Zoja and Donald Williams (Einsiedeln, Switzerland: Daimon Verlag, 2002), 119.

5. Ibid., 151.

6. Ibid., 152.

7. Ibid., 160.

8. Ibid., 173.

Notes to Chapter 5

1. Fouad Ajami, "Iraq and the Arabs' Future," *Foreign Affairs* 82, no. 1 (January–February 2003): 4.

2. United Nations Development Programme, *Arab Human Develop-*

ment Report 2002: Creating Opportunities for Future Generations (New York: Oxford University Press, 2003), 31.

3. Robert D. Kaplan, *The Coming Anarchy* (New York: Vintage Books, 2000), 100.

4. Ajami, "Iraq and the Arabs' Future," 3.

5. "PAS to Impose Islamic Laws If It Comes to Power," *Straits Times*, April 21, 2003, A5.

Notes to Chapter 6

1. Fareed Zakaria, *The Future of Freedom: Illiberal Democracy at Home and Abroad* (New York and London: Norton, 2003), 86.

2. Pang Eng Fong and Linda Lim, "Political Economy of a City-State," *Singapore Business Yearbook* (Singapore: Times Periodicals, 1982), 33.

3. Richard C. Paddock, "Asian Terrorist Network Growing," *Los Angeles Times*, June 22, 2003; available at www.latimes.com.

4. "Suspect Attended Bashir's School," *Straits Times*, August 11, 2003, A5.

5. "Bashir Warns of Divine Wrath," Streats, August 29, 2003, 60.

6. Meg Bortin, "Poll Shows U.S. Isolation: In War's Wake, Hostility and Mistrust," *International Herald Tribune*, June 4, 2003, 1.

7. "Saudi Leader Warns Against Backing Terrorists," *Los Angeles Times*, August 15, 2003; available at www.latimes.com.

8. John L. Esposito, *Unholy War: Terror in the Name of Islam* (New York: Oxford University Press, 2002), 138.

INDEX

151

INDEX

INDEX

INDEX

Mike Millard is a journalist who has lived and traveled in Asia for more than fifteen years, working for newspapers and international wire agencies.